G R O W U P

A Man's Guide to Masculine Emotional Intelligence

by
Owen Marcus

Copyeditor: Theresa Renner (www.germinatemediagroup.com)
Cover Design: Vanessa Maynard (www.vansessanoheart.net)
Cover Photo: curaphotography

Published in the United States by New Tribe Press
ISBN: 978-0-9887035-2-0

Table of Contents

GROW UP

A Man's Guide to Masculine Emotional Intelligence

Introduction

Are you the man you want to be?

Or do you feel buried under expectations, hopeless and paralyzed—like you'll never live up to your full potential?

You're not alone. As boys, we received more coaching on the fundamentals of football than we did on how to really *be* a man. But that just changed. Want to be a real man?

Here's your playbook.

As men, we weren't given all the tools we needed to be *real* men. *You* weren't given the tools to be the Remarkable Man you know is inside of you. But it isn't a psychological defect on your part; real manhood wasn't modeled for you. It wasn't taught to you. Our dads were out working, so our moms and predominantly female teachers were "raising" us. They taught us important lessons, but they couldn't teach us how to be real men.

I don't know about your dad, but mine came home tired from a long commute and vegged out in front of the TV. On the weekends, there was a lawn to mow and projects to do. "Emotional intimacy" wasn't my father's strong suit. How could he teach something he didn't know? Something that no one ever taught him?

Be your own man, not someone else's version of you

When you realize that some of your feelings, needs, and behaviors are not working in your life today because they're just vestiges of your childhood, it's very liberating. When you start to see how you inherited old models of masculinity... well, if you're like me, you get pissed. You might say, "I didn't sign up for this." I am not *your* man, I am *my* man!

This book is about learning how to be your own man. Rather than just continuing to accept the old model of manhood—or rebel against it—let's throw it out! Let's start over. Let's create what we want. Let's be *unreasonable!* Join me in defining what a Remarkable Man really is.

To become your own man you need to unlearn what was taught to you. Following the old model might get you everything you want—a family, success, power, money—but you'll give up full emotional expression and enjoyment. You'll give up thinking for yourself. You'll give up the power to freely say no. You'll give up your passion for a rich life. You'll give up developing your own Masculine Emotional Intelligence.

Life is an evolutionary process. As men, we often start the journey of change by attempting to solve a problem. Something's broken in your life, or you just can't see what's next. You try all your old tricks—the quickest, safest, and cheapest remedies. When they don't work, you finally look at things you never dreamt you'd consider: therapy, religion, support groups. If the pain is great enough, you'll try one.

In thirty-five years of discovering how to be my own man, I've seen a consistent pattern: a man will resist trying something new. Eventually, he'll actually do it, and get more than he expected. Suddenly, he's a huge champion of the solution. Ever had a friend tell you that you "have to" take yoga, start meditating, see this therapist or attend that church? He did and he feels better. He wants *you* to feel better, too.

Whatever approach you take, you learn to break out of your old boxes. Hopefully, you learn to let go of control and surrender to learning. If it works, you realize you've taught yourself a new strategy that goes beyond fixing: looking outside the existing box.

My stumbles

As a kid I was always different. I was a few steps behind the other kids. School, sports, and social interactions... no matter how hard I tried, I just couldn't keep up, let alone win. (Years later, I finally learned I had dyslexia and Asperger's syndrome. So not only were social interactions completely foreign to me, everything was backwards, too.)

Early on, I learned that since social interaction didn't come naturally to me, I needed to observe, analyze, and learn what others were doing. I'd take their behaviors apart like a mechanic disassembles an engine. I'd study how all the parts worked. Occasionally, I could figure something out and manage to replicate it, and that was the amazing part: sometimes it worked out. Sometimes the girl said yes to a date, sometimes I impressed the boss, sometimes the guys laughed at my jokes.

All my life I'd heard that a powerful man, a Remarkable Man, speaks the truth. My parents, my teachers, and television all reinforced that idea. As a child I thought, "OK, I get it. If people are going to respect me, I need to speak what is true. I can do that." That realization was empowering: it was something I could do, unlike so many other things I simply couldn't.

I was a bit of an instigator as a kid, so, armed with my belief that speaking the truth would earn me respect, I convinced my brother, my sister, and a few friends to go with me to knock on a neighbor's door. Mrs. Jones answered and faced me down. With my colleagues behind me, I blurted out my declaration: "No one likes you. You're mean. Stop picking on kids." I can't remember what happened next. Let's assume we ran.

That was a huge win. In the face of my fear, I spoke the collective truth, the truth others were not speaking. I was doing my family and the whole neighborhood a service. I felt great.

I went home later that afternoon to tell my mother about my act of courage. Of course, I didn't have to tell her; Mrs. Jones had already called. I was shocked when, instead of honor and respect from my parents, I got punishment—first from my mother, then from my father when he came home. It didn't make sense to me. I not only spoke my truth, I spoke the truth of all the adults. I should be thanked, right?

What initially felt like a win was, obviously, a huge failure. One of the characteristics of Asperger's is taking things literally. Gradually, I learned that what people said and what they actually believed were often different.

In spite of many more mishaps, I never gave up studying what it meant to be a Remarkable Man. If speaking the truth didn't make me a Remarkable Man, then what did? I read books on it. I watched my peers and other men try to discover the Remarkable Men inside of them.

Eventually, I realized something: no one had a clue. We were all winging it.

I didn't know if I felt relieved for not being as dumb as I thought I was, or hopeless, because obviously no one had figured it out. Either way, after this realization, I was even more committed.

It wasn't until I began my own journey in Boulder, Colorado, in the mid-1970s that I started to learn useful things about myself and how things really work. Every day I felt I was being shown more and more secrets. Part of me wanted to keep them to myself because I felt like I finally had an edge! But ultimately, I wanted to help set others free.

Throughout years of study, practice, and teaching, it all began to coalesce. I started to see simple patterns. These patterns could easily be learned by others, so I started teaching them to my clients, students, and men's group members. I continued to refine what I was learning through the teaching process.

I never imagined what my awkward childhood would lead to: me writing a book to help men learn what we were never taught. If I, the guy who struggled to learn *everything*, can learn this simple skill set to become comfortable in being the Remarkable Man I want to be, you can certainly learn these skills, too.

It will take commitment, practice, and acceptance—of yourself and others on their journeys. I want you to get it, so please use this book as your guide to filling the gaps in your Masculine Emotional Intelligence and to being that Remarkable Man you yearn to be. You can do it. This book will teach you how.

Embodying the powers of Masculine Emotional Intelligence

When we were in school, developing our emotional abilities never received the kind of support that developing our intellect did. We spend decades in school improving our intellect. How many years have you devoted to developing your emotional intelligence?

I doubt you ever attended a school for emotional development, earned a degree in it, and then made a living from it. If you are like most of us, you learned whatever you learned along the way.

Life experience is an excellent teacher. The problem is, that teacher wasn't always teaching you the best skills. Without formal teaching, or through inconsistent teaching and possibly poor instruction, the emotional intelligence you developed is much less than what you learned to develop intellectually.

This book doesn't go into the qualities of general emotional intelligence. There are many good books that do that, such as Daniel Goleman's *Emotional Intelligence*. Our focus is giving you a simple road map of how to fill in the gaps of what was missed. Your struggle with learning these emotional intelligence abilities has nothing to do with your competence. The problem is that what you needed wasn't there, or the environment wasn't favorable to learning.

Masculine Emotional Intelligence is not about being macho versus being sensitive; it's about being true to your unique emotional makeup—a makeup that is built on the general skills of emotional intelligence, yet is uniquely masculine.

As men, we appreciate good performance in ourselves and others. The growing body of research around emotional intelligence demonstrates that when you are functioning at a high level of emotional intelligence, you are outperforming your peers. Yet simple emotional intelligence skills such as empathy won't show up if you had no one modeling, teaching it, or even allowing it. These skills are innate in all humans, but they need fertile ground to grow.

Daniel Pink, bestselling author of *A Whole New Mind: Why Right-Brainers Will Rule the Future,* tells us that if we don't master these skills, we will be replaced by computers or outsourced labor. When you rely purely on your intellectual abilities, you are at risk of that knowledge and ability being replaced electronically. Emotional skills can't be transmitted over the Internet, no matter how hard we might try.

You can read about all the emotional traits such as listening, inspiring, guiding, vision, social and self-awareness skills, self-management, adaptability, and motivation. By mastering the foundation for these skills, you will successfully travel the path of these Nine Steps. Knowing what to do is different than doing it, though, isn't it? These skills must be learned experientially through focused practice and personal interaction.

Emotional intelligence is a better indicator for career success than traditional IQ.[1] Filling in the gaps of what was missed as you grew up will lead you to be that Remarkable Man you always wanted to be—probably with more success and joy.

Developing emotional intelligence will be the natural consequence of traveling these Nine Steps. Hell, you might become an elite athlete in the sport of emotional intelligence.

---

[1] Goleman, Daniel. "What Makes a Leader?" *Harvard Business Review,* January 1, 2004.

Why this book?

The old models haven't worked for a while. Part of the reason for our collective angst is that there has been no new model to attach our minds to. We are different men living in a different time. We want deeper relationships with our partners, we want more fulfilling work, we want to take a more active part in raising our kids, and we want to contribute to our communities and to the world. We want a life of meaning and purpose.

Beyond the benefit of fixing the issue that possibly had you purchase this book, there are numerous advantages to investing your time in the Nine Steps of Growing Up. You'll feel more connected to your partner and your kids. You'll have more clarity about who you are and what you really want. The concepts of "men" and "masculinity" are at a crossroads. We have evolved the macho side of ourselves for centuries. For the last few decades we've developed our sensitive side, largely because of women and their transformation. Now it is time to become Remarkable Men, where the best of the macho and the sensitive aspects come together to form a mature model of masculinity.

Growing up

In traditional cultures, the stages of growing up were well understood. The mythology, as well as the customs, were oriented towards guiding men to grow. The local tribe had ceremonies that not only marked transitions between particular stages, they provided follow-up support. These ceremonies would intensify what was occurring, or about to occur, then catalyze the needed shift. Guided and facilitated by the tribal elders, men were taken through a portal to a new place of personal masculinity.

In our culture, growing up just happens. You eat, sleep, and move, and your body grows. It's not treated as anything mystical or amazing. Your emotional growth "just happens" too. Life's circumstances will shape your development; how that shapes you, though, is determined by you. You can choose to be a victim of life, at the mercy of your circumstances... or you can choose to ride the wave and keep your head above the water.

I will always encourage you to stand up and ride your wave. In fact, *Remarkable Man* is mostly focused on giving you good instruction on how to best ride that wave. Over my thirty-five years of working with men and studying men from every angle I could find, I learned a few things. I learned the most from riding my own wave. I understood my falls and my wins because I studied them, shortening my learning curve. I hope to shorten your learning curve even more. I would have given a lot to have had a book like this when I was starting out.

It's not therapy

This book doesn't replace therapy. It might augment therapy. I have used a few therapists over the years as personal emotional trainers. When I found a good one, I studied and practiced with him, then took what I learned and applied it.

For me a good therapist is one who is healthy. A good therapist helps you complete what needs to be completed, while letting you drive the insights. The therapist can support you as he or she points out what you are not seeing or feeling. We can all get in a loop of sabotage by unconsciously denying what is occurring. More men are discovering coaches and men's groups that are giving them what they need. Get support. It makes it all quicker and easier.

In the resource section I discuss other therapies that I have seen. For many men, these were more useful than traditional psychotherapy. Take a risk; try a therapy you wouldn't normally try. If you want a different result, *do* something different. Be unreasonable. Step out of your box.

The three phases of change

Every transition has three parts. The first is the *separation* where the old is left behind. There is a small death of the past. Who you were will no longer exist in the same way. Often there is a biological analog to this evolutionary psychological change. Puberty is an excellent example of how the body, mind, and the collective work in sync. The boy is no longer a boy.

The second phase is the *challenge,* where the rebirth occurs. Once the old is dead and the attachments and identities to it are gone, there is space for a birth of a new man. The metamorphosis into a new stage is a discovery of a new self.

Once rebirth is complete the man is ready to *rejoin his community* as a new man. He is welcomed back, possibly with ceremonial celebration marking the transformation that occurred (think of that scene in *The Graduate*, where the protagonist's parents throw him a college graduation party, and all his father's friends give him unsolicited career advice). But often, men are just expected to suddenly rejoin society, and integrate themselves with no guidance or help whatsoever.
In today's culture these stages occur in isolation—as a boy with puberty and as a man with the other stages. Not only is the man not given guidance or any honoring, he is often shunned for being different because he changed.

With or without cultural support, men go through these transitions. They're real. They exist. You have, and will continue, to travel through these portals. Just as your biology changes, so does your consciousness. All this happens whether it's acknowledged by others, or you, or not.

You're not alone, though. There are thousands—millions?—of men all around the world going through the same things you are. If you don't have a group or place you can talk, find one. At the very least, come to www.owenmarcus.com and join the discussion. You don't have to do it alone.

The Nine Steps of Growing Up

You're not screwed up; you were never taught what you needed to learn. These Nine Steps offer you the opportunity to learn what you always wanted to know. The Nine Steps will give you the opportunity to become brilliant at Masculine Emotional Intelligence.

As men, you could say that we have holes, or spaces, inside of us that are left over from our incomplete experiences. In our society, we skip critical parts in our maturation because we were not given all the opportunities, support, or tools we needed to develop during that stage, and to therefore mature into real, adult men. These holes sabotage you by preventing you from being the Remarkable Man you want to be.

Even if the teaching or modeling was available, there was a good chance that because of stress, because of some level of trying to survive, you couldn't fully learn these skills. Who can learn when their parents are fighting and heading for a divorce? You only truly learn or heal when you are not in the stress or the survival response—when you are relaxed.

By becoming aware of these holes, and learning to fill them, you can mature. I discovered there are nine key places in our development that got skipped and need developing. Learning what you didn't learn will transform your life.

Here are the Nine Steps to Becoming the Remarkable Man you want to be:

1. Show up!
Being present gives you power.

2. If it ain't working, let it *die.*
Let go of what's not working so you have space for what can work.

3. Leave home—*really* leave home—and grow up.
Leave the dependency on women.

4. Ask for help: growing up is a community effort.
Who do you call at 2am when your world explodes?

5. Fill in the blanks.
Find what is undone in your life and finish it.

6. Man up! Take responsibility for yourself!
Develop the skills to live your life.

7. Go for it! Take some risks!
Take on an attitude of conscious risk.

8. Connect to the Divine, know you're not alone
Connect to something more than yourself.

9. Enjoy!
Receive your rewards.

With each step, there is a transition to the next. As you progress through the stages, the transitions become more subtle. I know from my own work, and working with thousands of men, that you can know all about how change occurs and still be surprised by how it manifests. Don't beat yourself up if, while working through these steps, you feel like you're in the middle of some chaos. You know what's great about chaos? It gets your attention away from the pattern in which you've been stuck. It rocks loose what was holding you tight. It also takes you out of your head so it is easy to forget what you wanted to unlearn anyway.

Because these Nine Steps are steps of personal evolution, a young man will not be focusing on the later stages. He can incorporate aspects of later stages, but if you are in your twenties, don't be concerned about receiving all the rewards of your life yet. Your focus at that age will be living it; going for the adventure life brings you. Use this book to receive the full joy of the moment.

I emphasize the importance of allowing the Nine Steps to unfold naturally because I have seen men attempt to grow up too soon. Not only did that backfire in terms of their development, it was less fun. Much of growing is taking risks and making mistakes. Thinking and planning too much takes you out of the moment and your life. I am saying particularly to the younger men: allow yourself to be a little immature. This book is a map; go off the trail occasionally to explore the local environs.

Women and this book

Women are crazy!

How many times have you said that? I know I have countless times. They're so emotional. Don't you hate that... don't you love that? Women are erratic, irrational—they are not men. And they can keep us honest.

As you read the book you will increase your appreciation for being a man, and consequently, your appreciation for women. I have seen this, and I have heard it over and over again in men's groups: as you learn to express your emotions in an honest, masculine way, she won't be so "irrational" with her emotions.

At first she may test you with more irrationality, but as you use that part of you more, she won't have to be the sole source of emotions in the relationship. When you refuse to feel and express, it's as though you *force* your partner to do it for you. As you get more honest, she can be, too. She'll like that as much as you do.

We have more in common with women than we don't. Yet there are distinctions to emotional intelligence that are unique to men—and to you. As you read the Nine Steps, you will realize how you can be emotional in ways that are more natural for you. As you develop your Masculine Emotional Intelligence, you will also find that women will appreciate you more.

As you begin to understand Masculine Emotional Intelligence, you will realize that not only was your emotional education primarily from women, so was society's. Since we left the tribe for the farm 10,000 years ago, men have been progressively less available to raise children. As women stepped up to raise the children all on their own, they also stepped up to teach the emotional roles of the family and culture. Slowly, we relinquished emotionality to the female gender.

This gradual shift in what it means to be emotional naturally took a feminine slant. So when a woman tells you she needs you to "be emotional," realize that what she's asking for may be skewed toward the feminine—and she probably doesn't even realize that. Your resistance is actually more than just fear and not wanting to give up control; it's because you *can't* meet her requests because her suggestions don't fit for a man.

But ladies, this is *not* a Fix Your Man manual. Men and women are *very* different, and even when he's changed, he's not going to be your best girlfriend. The emotional intimacy is different. You will always need your "girlfriends;" he will always need his buddies. Men and women are different.

As I was writing this book I was constantly told by women, "I need to give this to my friend/lover/husband/brother/son/ nephew!" Great, I'd say. But here's the caveat: if you give it to a man to make your point that he is messed up, he won't read it. If you give it to him as an instruction manual to fix what you think is broken, he won't read it.

My suggestion is that you use the book as a way to open a new conversation about your relationship. You might want to read the book yourself first to better understand men—or, even better, show him you *want* to better understand men.

A man can say he wants to be a better man, but men don't like to take on tasks we can't succeed at, so give him the book as a way to win.

My suggestion is that you support him in learning and practicing these new skills. Emphasize his wins. It can be slow at first. I've noticed that men might not initially do it for themselves; they may embark on this journey for their partner and their kids. It's hard for us to give ourselves the gift of being our own man.

My other suggestion is that you support him in getting support outside of your relationship. Make it easy for him to spend time with supportive friends, or even a men's group. Reading the book will help, but having men to support him will accelerate this change and lessen your load.

Men need "guy time" doing fun things: sports, gaming, fixing cars, fishing, whatever. But it doesn't necessarily meet emotional needs. They need quality time with men. Just like with you and your girlfriends; sometimes you just want to shop, or grab lunch, and sometimes you need time and space to really emotionally connect with your friends. So allow him that time and space.

You may be thinking, "I don't want him to be with a group of guys bashing women!" Neither do I. My experience with the men's groups I've known is that men *support* women; often a man's group is telling him what his wife has told him for years! We just are able hear it better from our peers.

There are many aspects of this book that are applicable to women, too, of course. Given that we are still living in a masculine-dominated culture, this book will give you insight into our entire culture.

This book is not about creating a split between men and women. When a man steps deeper into being a man, he is more present for women. Like learning anything, there may be some rough spots as a man learns to feel, express, and do new things. The book is not about seeing men or women as victims of each other or of life. It is about the co-creation of Remarkable Men.

Boys and this book

One question I get from both men and women is how to use this book for boys. This book is definitely appropriate for boys. For preteens, I suggest you read it, adapt what's appropriate, and discuss it with your son.

Teenagers want to be adults, and they want respect. They believe at some magical point they will suddenly be adults. And when that doesn't happen, a young man thinks there's something wrong with *him*. Give him this book to show him that being a man is about always learning and growing, always growing up. If someone had told me that, it would have saved me a lot of grief.

Please don't treat this book as a to-do list for your son. This book is about growing up as a man, and young men haven't had all the experiences that will shape them. Explain that it's less a training manual and more about what's possible. Just learning that men don't have it all figured out is very powerful for a young man.

How to use this book

I know how it is. You read an article or a book that contains interesting prospects. You think, "I didn't know that, I can use that," and you do. I hope this book does that for you. I want this book to be more than intellectual entertainment. I want you to experiment with what is written. See what is true for you. Apply the principles and behaviors. Discuss what you are learning with your partner, your friends, and co-workers. If you are brave, take on a few of the tasks and have someone hold you accountable for achieving them.

Remember: it's not about getting it right, it's about learning. You want to be a better man, you want a better life for yourself and family—you need to have a plan and start working that plan. The plan will probably change once you start. But nothing will change unless you start.

Get feedback. Use what you are learning as you observe other men. In an accepting manner see how they are, in some way, like you. Often you will learn much from first seeing a phenomenon in another.

Make it a team sport. Join or create a men's group so you can practice with other men. Use the book as more than a discussion point; use it as a study guide. See the resources in the appendix for more help in applying what you're learning. I know of no better way to speed up your change, make it on the whole easier and have more fun at it than to do it with a group. Let the book upset you. It could make you sad or it might piss you off—great! Take that emotion and put it into an action. Create a personal manifesto from the book. Create your own business plan for becoming the man you want to be. Write it down. Share it. Post it on our website, www.owenmarcus.com.

Take a stand for being that man. Be willing to be seen as "unreasonable." Share your story on the site. Support other men. That is not only very rewarding, it is also a way to take a short cut to growing up. And a way to educate: women, you can share your perspective.

We can go on about the assumptions of what a man is and what masculinity is. I would rather give you ways to create that shift to being the man you want to be. My intent in addressing masculinity was to start to put some cracks in your box of what it means to be a man and give you the seeds to grow your own personal model of masculinity. Fill that new model with what you learn from reading and practicing the principles of this book. Let your experience be your teacher.

Bottom line: you are not bad, wrong, or dumb. You were never taught what is in this book. You have lived someone else's life long enough. Now you get to live your own life. Working on your personal growth is not only admirable, it is necessary today. The edge in today's market is maturity and Masculine Emotional Intelligence.

"Sober" up

Addictions are an escape from reality. If you are an addict, stop here. The rest will be just a game. Don't waste your time. Sure, you might get some value, but you'll keep coming back to your addiction. I am not going to guide you through your addiction. This book is not about addictions. It's about growing up. You can't grow up if you're an addict who's still using.

Our men's group will not allow a man to participate who is an addict until he has sobered up. Whether he was addicted to drugs, alcohol, gambling, sex, whatever, he has to have given up using his drug of choice if he wants to participate in our men's group.

Until you are sober, you *are* your drug(s). You can't be present with a drug in your body. You can't truly love when your true love is a drug. You can't keep your word when you serve your drug. You can't grow up as a man.

Every addict or ex-addict I have known is brilliant, caring, and highly sensitive, which I suspect explains part of the reason he became an addict. Because of that brilliance, he is highly skilled at bullshitting first himself, and then others. He has become the master of lies. He got very good at fooling everyone through his victimhood, charm, success, and deception.

I will grant you that we all, in some form, now have or have had obsessions or escapes. When I say "addiction," I'm talking about being addicted to a substance or dangerous behavior. As long as that substance or behavior determines what you will do, you are addicted. There are gray areas, like cigarettes; their impact is not like alcohol or drugs. If you want to raise your bar on growing up, however, give up smoking.

As with all addictions and the distracting behaviors associated with them, when you begin to give them up, many of the old feelings you suppressed with the substance start to come up. The substance is the pacifier to placate the emotions or needs that you don't want to feel or express. As your drug leaves, you can begin to address the real issues. The drug is a distraction. Go to the source and you will cure the addiction and more.

Do the hardest thing you have ever done: get sober. The courage that it takes to face your addiction will empower you, and be a huge gift to yourself and others. Treatment has come a long way. If you are willing to do what it takes, treatment will work.

The men whom I have seen get on the other side of this are some of the most beautiful people I have ever met. The compassion and courage they learned from their journey with addiction is a gift to the world. When you kill this beast... you are *fearless*!

A few notes

I have changed the names of the men I use as examples and, where appropriate, a few of the details to protect their identities. Again, please don't see the book or the Nine Steps as rigid steps. They are in a relative order, but the order can vary per man. Also, a few stages can be affecting you simultaneously. If you can keep your focus on a stage and you want to take on another, go for it.

Ultimately, it is *you* that you are seeking. Use the Nine Steps to introduce yourself to your own unique, beautiful, strong, confident self. Change it up. Invent new practices. Tweak the ones I've given you until they fit you perfectly. You're the director of your own maturity now. I am eagerly anticipating your special, distinctive process and intend that you experience both extraordinary benefit as well as pleasure from my offering.

Owen Marcus

Disclaimer

Consult your own physician or licensed healthcare practitioner regarding the applicability of any opinions or recommendations with respect to your symptoms or medical/psychological condition. Information shared in this book and on websites or personally is shared for educational purposes.

This information is not to be used to diagnose, treat, cure, or prevent a disease. Owen Marcus is not a medical doctor.

Chapter 1:
Show Up

"To be yourself in a world that is constantly trying to make you something else is the greatest accomplishment."

—Ralph Waldo Emerson

Being present gives you power

Slow down.

Right now. Just slow down. Take a deep breath. Just be present with yourself.

Why? Because it allows you to connect with yourself. Another way to say that is that it creates mindfulness. Mindfulness allows for presence. Presence is the key to being Remarkable. In other words, get real.

Feel what you really want. See where you really want to go. Know who you really want to be.

This is the first of the Nine Stages, so let's set an intent right now: be present, be mindful. Don't worry about doing it right, just *try*.

What do you really want?

What do you want? When you think of "growing up," what does that mean for you? Beyond what you want to fix in yourself, what do you want to create in your life? What old forgotten dream have you buried that still smolders with embers of passion?

It may be something that's not achievable anymore—pitching in a World Series game *might* not be realistic for you. It may even be something you don't *want* anymore; maybe climbing Mount Everest has lost its appeal. But use that dream, that old passion, to help you remember (or experience for the first time) an emotion essential to growing up: hope.

Hope, and focus, will give you passion and motivation to move through the tough times.

Keep asking yourself what you want as you become more present. You will probably feel old pain and thoughts come up, but just keep focusing on your intent to be more present. Teach yourself the ability to have dual attention: fully experience the present *and* maintain a focus on what you want. To do that, you will need to experience, accept, and let go of what is occurring in the present moment: what you're feeling, what you're thinking, and the judgments you're passing on yourself and others. See it all, acknowledge it, then *let it all go*. That's how you stay present.

Your unconscious is powerful. Get it working for you. As you begin to get a picture or feeling of what you truly want, write about it. If you're not a writer, create a collage as your vision board. Do whatever you need to do to create a record of what you want. Maybe you leave yourself a voicemail on your phone.—that's simple and easy to do. Listen to it every day. Maybe you buy a plant and use it as a symbol of how your dream will grow. Water it; put it in the sun. Even a Post-It on your dashboard or bathroom mirror will alert your unconscious to focus on what you want.

NOTE: Don't use day-dreaming about your intent as an escape from what you are really experiencing. Not only are you less likely to get what you want just by dreaming, but even if you were to get it, you are less likely to fully enjoy it. Or worse: you might find it's not what you wanted after all. It would be like sleeping as your friend drives your car and waking up at the wrong destination. You might have told your friend where you wanted to go, but you didn't direct him.

Simple skill, powerful effects

Sally was a woman who worked for a large corporation. She was on four medications for her high blood pressure, but even with all the meds, she was rushed to the hospital twice in one year. Her boss was so concerned for her health, he sent her to me.

I was teaching Mindfulness-Based Stress Reduction (MBSR) at the time. The popularity of Mindfulness is in large part due to Dr. Jon Kabat-Zinn, the author of several books on Mindfulness and creator of MBSR. Jon took the simple yet sophisticated practice of being present in the moment and developed a remedial program for us stressed-out Westerners.

He didn't teach the philosophy behind it; you don't need to really understand that for it to work. You just need to do it, and Dr. Kabat-Zinn teaches how to do it in such a way that in just eight weeks, severely stressed patients can heal themselves of conditions no drug can fix.

The philosophy behind it is simple: in short, we're not cavemen anymore. We don't have saber-tooth tigers hunting us, yet our DNA is programmed for exactly that. We don't generally face life-threatening situations every day, but our bodies can't tell the difference between our brains saying, "That mammoth is going to stomp me," and "If I don't meet this deadline, I may get fired." To our bodies, it's *all* stress.

In some ways, cavemen had it easier: once they safely got away from that mammoth, their stress response shut off. In today's world, there is *always* a new deadline, a mortgage to pay, traffic to fight, etc. Consequently, your stress response is always "on." But that is a *learned behavior*. You never told your brain, "a missed deadline will not make me saber-tooth chow," so your body perceives *all* stress as life-or-death, and puts you in a fight-or-flight response.

So unlearn it. You can turn off that constant stress response. Teach your mind and body *not* to be constantly stuck in survival mode. That's what Mindfulness-Based Stress Reduction teaches.

When you learn *not* to constantly exist in a stress reaction mode, you are in the *present moment*. In the present moment, you have access to your full array of resources—mental, emotional, physical, sexual, and spiritual. You're not just more relaxed, you are more creative and able to perform at your best.

Back to Sally. In her pre-course interview, she said she couldn't possibly do the homework for our course, which was 45 minutes of mindfulness exercises a day. She simply didn't have the time. She was *far* too busy meeting deadlines. I told her to just try.

By her post-course interview, Sally was off all her meds, her blood pressure was normal, she enjoyed work, and she had renewed a relationship with her estranged son. All of this was corroborated by her boss who added that her co-workers liked her once again.

I haven't taught this course in years, but I still highly recommend it. Aside from countless anecdotes like Sally's, there's growing clinical research that supports the efficacy of MBSR[2]. By being aware of what is occurring in you and outside of you, without being in reaction mode, you get to just *be*. In our culture, in part because we tend not to be present in the moment, we are encouraged to focus on *doing* and *having* to the exclusion of *being*.

---

[2] www.mindfulexperience.org a site with up to date research on Mindfulness

Just *breathe*. The core of MBSR is breathing. After a few weeks in class, people would invariably share how they caught themselves not breathing when they thought they were relaxed! Breath is something we take for granted, but I had clients who were Olympic marathon runners who realized they were not breathing to their full capacity.

So *breathe*.

Train yourself to breathe when you are not stressed. If you aren't doing it when you're relaxed, you certainly won't do it while stressed. Take a Mindfulness-Based Stress Reduction course. They are readily available and often paid for by insurance providers.

Use the power of your body

When you go through life without the base or foundation of being present, you are going through life asleep at the wheel. You're not much more than a robot. There is no way you will grow up, or ever be truly happy, if you're not present.

So if you're not present, where are you? Who are you?

I'm sure you've known men who invest a lot of energy and money into their image—only to have it work *too* well. They buy the right clothes, cars, and houses to get the right spouse, job, and life. One day they wake up, maybe only briefly, look in the mirror, and see a face looking back they don't recognize. Who the hell is that person? They remember the boy or young man who had passion and a dream, but see a man who sold out. He has a wife and kids and a career—and a life that is not serving him. Then the question becomes: will he go back to sleep, or will he fight to stay awake?

A man's story

Many years ago, Sam came to see me for Rolfing® Structural Integration[3] (SI), the soft tissue manipulation oriented towards releasing chronic tension that I have been practicing for more than thirty years. Sam was a pediatric neurologist who had achieved success at a relatively young age for a doctor. He had the added advantage of being good-looking and a natural athlete. He was the guy everyone wants to be. In the course of going through the series of ten Rolfing® (SI) sessions, Sam started to relax. He started to come down from a life of always doing. One day near the end of the series of Rolfing® (SI) sessions, he came in with a relaxed look on his face. I asked him what was up. He told me he was going to quit practicing medicine.

A few days earlier, Sam got up and knew he was done with the medical profession. But rather than feeling fear or panic, he felt a calm he hadn't felt in years. Sam explained that being a doctor was never his idea; it was his parents'. He thought it sounded good and didn't want to disappoint them, so he went for it.

His plan was to finish his commitment with the hospital, then to take the time he never had to explore what he wanted. I never heard where he ended up. I wasn't concerned, though. I knew he would find what was true for him. I knew what courage it took to step away from that perfect career, after all he had invested—and I knew that courage would lead him to what was right for him. I am honored to have known Sam.

---

[3] Rolfing Structural Integration (SI) is a form of soft tissue manipulation focus on releasing chronic stress and tension to structurally align the body. It is usually a series of ten sessions. For more information, go to www.rolf.org.

Are you that man? Have you had a moment of mindfulness, a moment of truly being present, when you wondered how the hell you got to be who you are? If so, congratulations! You are being honest. You are being mindful to the truth of your life. That's not easy.

When you're not experiencing your body anymore

Bodies don't get enough respect. We use them and abuse them. We're better at maintaining cars than our bodies.

Through your body you will become aware. MBSR is so successful in part because it starts with the body and not the mind. Students practice a body scan that slowly talks them through their bodies. They learn about their bodies and learn how to relax. Eventually, they use their bodies as an ever-present biofeedback system. Do you feel tense? Shoulders tight? *Breathe.* Are your hands cramping up? *Get off the computer for a few minutes!* Feel lethargic and tired? *Sit up straight and breathe!*

Through becoming aware of what your body is experiencing, you will pick up subtler and subtler clues about who you are being. You will become more sensitive to what is already occurring. You will feel how your body is tensing. That's your body's way of telling you something is off. As you experience the discomfort and learn to read what it means, you will understand when your body is telling you that the current situation is toxic, or when you are having an unwarranted stress reaction. This will empower you to be true to yourself by first learning what is true for you. If your body is getting tense, you need to learn to listen to what it's saying. Are you too attached to a certain outcome? Do you have tunnel vision so you're unaware of other options?

Thirty-five years ago, I was completely unaware and going from one reaction to another. Through listening to my body first, I learned things I didn't want to know. I learned how much I held in my emotional expression, in particular my anger. My body's responses taught me to feel, accept, and then express. With the help of body therapies, my tension and anger were physically worked out of my body and dissipated. Do I still get tense? Of course! But I don't let it send me into a fight-or-flight response. Do I still feel anger? Of course! But I know the anger is genuinely about what is *right* in front of me, in the present moment. It's not leftover from something I didn't fully process twenty years ago.

Do what you need to do to "be in your body." Rather than thinking too hard about what you're feeling, just feel your body. Scan your body, notice what's happening. After a while you will hear your body speaking without needing to ask. Go out and get some good bodywork to aid the release of the old tension. Good bodywork is the short course for learning how to listen and how to grow up, because it releases so much old tension and old emotion.

Once you are in your body, your mother isn't. What does that mean? Well, as a boy you are deeply connected to your mother, first in her womb and then through your nursing and finally through your development as a child. Men often fill that need—someone taking care of their physical needs—with their wives, sometimes their doctors, even their favorite take-out places (even though fast food doesn't love you back). Leaving childhood behind means letting go of having someone or something else take care of your body. It means learning to be fully responsible for your own body.

To be responsible for your body, you need to be aware of it. A mature man is *in* his body. He's connected to all aspects of himself. He's not "checked out;" he is present. If you're tense, you're not present. Others will not fully trust you, because clearly, you don't fully trust your own experience—or you would be relaxed.

Change your body... change your mind

Your body is a literal metaphor for who you are as a man. It's no accident that you have the body you have. Sure, your hair and eye color, your general height, and your blood type are genetic. But the quality of your body patterns—its tension, structure (or posture), and movement—are learned. Over a lifetime, your body adapts to stress. As a child you learn to survive stress in the best way you can. Generally speaking, you either model your parents or go in the complete opposite direction of their adaptive pattern. For instance, if your father was mean or just overbearing, you had two basic choices: be a bully like him, or a wimp who doesn't stand up for himself. This might sound a little oversimplified, but that's what we do when we are in survival mode.

Now, the idea that the survival choices we made actually translated into our body structure may seem a little out there, but go with me for a minute: let's say you dealt with stress at home by being a bully at school. If so, you might have developed a large chest. If you retreated from the conflict, you might have a smaller chest. People might have said you inherited your big chest from your father. I will say that you developed that chest by unconsciously modeling your father's behavior of how to deal with stress—right down to his body structure.

Again, I know it sounds a little out there. But you don't have to trust me; do your own experiment. Let's stick with the big chest versus the small chest for the experiment. First, walk around a room with your chest puffed out as much as possible. You shoulders are back, your head is up, your gait is strong. As you do this, start describing your day. Feel what this feels like.

Notice what behaviors suddenly feel natural. What do you want to do now?

Now, go back to your normal posture for a minute, and then take on the small chest posture. This time focus more on exhaling, keeping your chest small. Hunch over and look down as you walk around speaking about your day. Listen to your words *and* their tone. Now what do you want to do?

Comparing the two—chest puffed out, chest collapsed—where are you more and less social? With each posture, what is your predominate emotion? Sadness, fear, anger, shame, or joy?

Much more than you realize, your body and mind were imprinted on you as a child. The imprinters didn't know they were doing it. You certainly didn't know it. It was a combination of you being indirectly guided and using the best skill you had to adapt to your stress.

Everyone grew up with this phenomenon, yet we don't realize the impact this body/mind conditioning had, and still has, on us. The quality of your body's stress, and its response to past stress, becomes something like a computer virus that corrupts your present moments. You don't know it because this reality is the only reality you know, like a fish who doesn't know it's swimming in water until you take it out because there was never any "not water" to compare it to. You don't realize your physiology and your thoughts are emanating from the unconscious organization of your body.

Your past, via your body, is keeping you from being fully present. At best, the computer virus of old tension is replicating your past in your present, much like the war veteran who dives under the table when a car backfires. In some cases, people become completely addicted to stress and its adrenaline; but in all cases, we are at least unconsciously conditioned.

I know this picture of being a victim to your past stress sounds like the complete *opposite* of empowering, but there are many ways to excise your past. The exercises at the end of this chapter, as well as the resource chapter at the end of this book, will give you many options.

The best place to start, however, is with bodywork. Your body is malleable. You can change it. You can remove that ever-present pull to recreate your past. You can release the deep tension in your body through bodywork. You can train your body and your mind how *not* to go into the stress response. You can sculpt a new body as well as a new life. You can develop a backbone that is not rigid, per se, but strong and sustainable. And you can experience the beauty of simple pleasures your body can give you when it's relaxed.

Don't fix; be

OK, you're a guy. So you like to give advice and fix things. We all do. And that's not bad. Women can love us for that. The downside is that you can use that need to fix and give advice as a way to escape, or not be present with yourself or someone else. Women—friends and lovers—have asked me to just listen and feel.

As a boy, how often were you just accepted for who you were without needing to perform? Is it possible your rush to fix things comes from memories of being given attention when you were a boy for what you *did*, rather than just who you *were*?

Regardless of who does or doesn't accept you now, you need to accept yourself. All those little behaviors you learned were ways to distract yourself from what was really happening, and therefore have prevented you from growing up. As you give up the need to do those things, and surrender to your experience, you will grow up more than most men.

There's a good chance you will be dropping some masks you wore that helped create your success. Masks are faces we put on to conceal the real one. That surrender can be scary as you feel vulnerable and sort of "naked" without the ways you used to hide yourself. You may feel grief from the loss of these personas, which have become old friends. On some level, you may believe that your mask, that part of your personality you project to the world, *was* you, the real you—and the key to your success. It might have been a component to your success, but it is certainly not you.

Allow your mind to go back to the innocence of a child. How does that feel? It doesn't mean you have to be naïve. You are just developing what the Buddhists call the Beginner's Mind: that state of being when you are open to new experiences.

Notice when you have that urge to fix something and before you jump in, take a moment to get present. Ask yourself what you are feeling. What do you really want? Get honest. In men's groups, a new man may try to jump in to fix or rescue another man who is having a difficult time. The group stops the process to suggest to the fixer that what he wants to fix or rescue in the other man is most likely in him. In other words, rather than just hang with what is occurring, the new man wants to divert his agitation by helping another man.

You want *something*. We all do. Figure out what it is, and determine your best action to get what you want—while staying mindful. First, focus on your feeling and needs, before jumping in to try to provide what others need.

A man's story

Dean came to me for Rolfing® (SI) because of his chronic back problem. Back problems are generally easy fixes, and Dean's was no exception. As with many of my clients, though, he brought a deeper challenge to me.

Dean owned a successful chiropractic practice that he had worked hard to create. He was an effective salesman, and he was always on. Always being on was a lot of work—it created the constant tension that caused his back problem. When Dean's body and back started relaxing his "always on" started to relax. At first he loved it. He was sleeping better, his running improved, and he was having the best sex of his life.

The intense drive to keep producing and selling started to relax. After a couple of weeks of that, his office manager said, "Dean, what's wrong with you? You don't seem so driven. You aren't working so hard. You aren't going for every opportunity. Fewer patients are coming in." His businesses dropped. What surprised Dean more than anything was that he wasn't panicking—at first. Dean asked if he would get his "mojo" back. I said yes, but that it would be different.

After a few more weeks Dean's passion for work returned, and this time, he found himself being more genuine. He wasn't selling to his patients, he was relating to them. He was speaking less and listening more. He wasn't working as hard but was getting the same results. He wasn't jumping in trying to immediately fix or give advice.

Dean's back problems never returned. His mask of always being on, always selling, softened. His patients were less like customers and more like friends. His practice was successful, not because he was doing a good job selling, but because he was being with his patients. The need to always fix the immediate crisis in order to be of value evolved into co-creating sustainable health for his clients. His clients saw him less often, but sent him more clients because they liked him.

For us men, decreasing our need to perform and fix is a new concept. "Just being" is a new concept, too. We don't have many models of how to do that, or concrete proof of why it actually works better. Women have been conditioned to this "fix-it" mindset just as much as we have, but with a slightly different slant. They will directly or indirectly ask for something to be fixed when what they really want is to be with us. As you become more aware of your fix-it pattern, you will let it go, and shift to relating to people, not trying to solve their problems.

Breaking any pattern can be uncomfortable at first. Hang in there. Take a risk. Go for communication and intimacy instead. In the long run, you and everyone you deal with will appreciate it.

Hold the space

I am still working on my mastery of this concept. But the crux of it is this: if you can stay present with your emotions while standing in your truth, you are being a man.

Holding space is the ability to create an emotionally and physically safe atmosphere. It is the feeling someone gets that allows them to let down their guard. Most people will not let down their guard until you do. I'm not suggesting that you become a wimp here; part of creating a safe space for yourself and others is your willingness to take a stand when necessary. You know the difference between walking into a room where someone is pissed, and walking into a room where that same person is open. In the first scenario you show up defensively, and in the second you are relaxed, looking forward to the interaction.

The ability to hold emotional and physical space comes with being mindful. You will not possess the power needed to hold the space for others if you can't hold it for yourself. So be present for yourself—you need to be mindful and accepting of what is occurring for you.

When you can take that openness into a stressful situation, you hold the space for others to stay more open. Maintaining the focus and openness when chaos is occurring is a strong masculine quality. Women gravitate to a man who is relaxed, open, and focused when others aren't. Other men trust that man. They see that, under pressure, he does not pass the buck of stress to someone else. He holds his space of relaxed focus. That shows other men that he can be trusted, and he will honor his word. When he says that he will do something, he will do it—even when the shit is hitting the fan.

The man who holds the space is willing to risk relationships for the truth, because he knows without truth there is no true relationship. He knows that speaking the unspeakable sets everyone free, including himself.

Are you willing to face the threat of collapse to stand in the truth of the moment? Are you willing to allow yourself to feel your feelings? If you can stay present with your emotions while standing in your truth, you are being a man. You are willing to be and do the right thing regardless of the consequence. You serve the truth. As a good king would, you serve a higher source: your truth and those in your kingdom. True power is being fully present no matter what is occurring.

You have been tested. You will be tested. You have failed; you will fail again. That is learning. Growing is using your failure as an awareness exercise—so that the next time, you are different.

Here is a secret to succeeding the next time: forgive yourself. Accept your failure with compassion. That same compassion you might not have been given when you were a boy; the compassion you would want to give your son. Denying, stuffing, or pushing down your emotions will sabotage you. Those unacknowledged emotions will rear their ugly heads when you least want them to.

Here is a tip: focus on your vision of the man you want to be. Put that in the space you hold for yourself and others. When you see or feel that vision weaken, it is a clue that you are "checking out," becoming unconscious and not mindful. Come back to that vision as you come back to your experience. With both of them present, breathe. Then you can step forward into the space as a warrior for truth.

One question I ask myself about how I should respond to a situation is whether a particular action will take or give me energy. In the long run, will I be more myself, more mature, more powerful if I do that particular act? The question is not much different than asking, "if I go out for a run will I feel better afterward?" This question will help you take the long view. It will help you see the full effect of your actions. It will have you asking whether this action is furthering you in being the man you want to be. If the action in question serves that deeper part of you, not the superficial masks, it will be right for all.

Others will often object to your growth. In my personal and professional experience, there will always be people who are threatened by this deep change. By virtue of your changing they feel pressure on themselves to change—even if you never bring it up or discuss it with them. You've heard the old adage about "crabs in a bucket"? In a bucket full of crabs, if one crab tries to escape, the others will pull it back down. You may have friends, family, or coworkers like that—they would rather prevent you from growing than grow themselves.

When I first heard this Buddhist statement I questioned it: "There is only one right action and it is the right action for everyone." I see it now, though. Truth is truth for everyone. Others might not like it, but it doesn't make it less true.

At the end of the day you might not have achieved your goal, but you were being a man for fully showing up. You were true to yourself and your vision of yourself. You gave yourself a huge gift. You accepted yourself when others might not have. Keep this up; you will grow up. If you do no other step, do this one. This one will lead you to and through the rest.

It was a little over ten years ago that I realized I had Asperger's Syndrome—which explained many of my behaviors as a kid. One of the blessings of having Asperger's is that you speak your mind! As my example in the introduction illustrates, my innate need to speak up could get me in trouble. What these "screw-ups" taught me was that speaking up and getting in trouble would never kill me. I wasn't any braver than my friends, but because I had to speak I learned that speaking the truth as best as I could would set myself, and others, free.

I still have not learned to shut up, but I have had my struggles with *speaking* up. One such struggle occurred when a respected teacher of mine betrayed his word not only to me, but to those under my tutelage. I naïvely questioned why he was behaving in a manner I hadn't seen before. He gave me some reasons. Respecting him and liking him, I believed him. These reasons did not prove to be true.

A few weeks later I was in a business meeting with my colleagues. Suddenly, out of the blue, I was being drilled by a few of them. My first response was to freeze and be silent. My actions and intents were being impugned. Others, who had previously expressed to me concerns similar to mine with this teacher, were now attacking me, or acting as if we never had those conversations.

On the inside I was shaking. I felt as if it was obvious to others, and maybe it was. I wanted to kill and run and cry at the same time. All the worst symptoms of my Asperger's and my dyslexia were present. When I got a few words out, they were not clear. I felt like a cornered animal.

After hearing a voice in my head say, "You are *fucked*," I heard another voice tell me to use this as learning and healing. I told myself I had nothing to lose. I began to speak what was true for me. I am sure it was far from articulate, but it was authentic. All the built-up energy started to move through me. I let my body express what was going on. I let my voice crack. I spoke.

My speaking the unspeakable broke loose what kept me quiet those times before when I didn't speak. It showed me that the truth would set me free. Within six months of this event, this former teacher and many of the associates had moved away. Some of the silent people were thanking me for speaking up. I realized I could have spoken up sooner. I forgave myself for being silent. Most of all, I was free.

Years later, I can see how this crisis was one of the seeds for me to teach other men to speak what they feel they can't. This experience and similar ones taught me what no one else was teaching me. They taught me what it was to hold the space for myself and truth.

Putting it all together

So a whole chapter on being present—that's a lot of writing about something so seemingly simple. Yes, it is simple, but not always easy. Practicing in order to develop this skill will transform your life. In the moment, you will be able to release what would have taken you out of the moment. Rather than run from the thought, sensation, or emotion, you become aware of it and let go of it.

When you do these *micro releases* a few thousand times over several months in all those moments of mini-stress, panic, or survival, I guarantee that you will be a different man. More than any other method this will surely strengthen you in being a Remarkable Man. Do it enough and this behavior will become your default response under stress. Think about how that alone will impact your life.

In practicing being present and holding space, you are learning the most basic Masculine Emotional Intelligence skill. It's a skill that boys should have been taught but weren't; it's a skill that allows you to shift from being just along for the ride with your emotions to capitalizing on their power. Men who "fly off the handle" or "have anger control issues" are using the excuse that they couldn't help themselves. Bullshit. Real men know that having emotions is part of being a real man. For example, if being angry scares you, you may avoid situations that provoke anger; in doing that, however, you will also be more likely to allow others to violate your boundaries. Slowly accepting your anger will allow you to let go of it when it doesn't serve you, and express it when it does.

In all aspects of being present, you are in many ways giving yourself what you didn't get as a child. You are giving yourself acceptance and self-love. You are teaching yourself that you don't need to do things to be accepted. Being accepted for simply being begins with you accepting yourself and your body *as they are.*

Once you have a foothold on self-acceptance, you start to hold that state in more and more challenging situations, building the muscles of that acceptance, so that you are a powerful man holding that space and allowing others to step into it themselves.

Those dreams of yours that were disparaged by others—and even yourself—can start to have an environment in which to germinate and grow into aspects of yourself that are new to you. It is as if the *hungry ghosts* (another Buddhist saying, meaning those unmet needs and insatiable desires) are being fed so they can let go. Buried in your unconscious and your body are these legitimate feelings and needs that were denied. The acceptance of this allows you to expand the depth of your life in the present and makes space for true maturity.

You may not have gotten what you wanted and needed as a kid. But as your mindfulness of what you want and need *now* increases and as these needs are satiated, you will be more available to develop the other eight steps. As you *just be* with who you are now, you are ready to go through your own rites of passage from the child to the adult. Without being embodied in who you are, without beginning to accept who you are as a man, the other steps won't be powerful or sustainable. Before you can move forward, you need to be where you are and take the first step from there. You wouldn't begin a journey from Los Angeles to New York by starting in Omaha. That would be impossible. Begin where you are. From there you have choice. There are many roads from L.A. to N.Y.

Remarkable Tasks
The following are exercises to learn, reinforce, and embody your growth as a Remarkable Man.

Learning to breathe
I have worked with thousands of clients, including professional athletes, who don't breathe to their fullest capacity. It is not about taking a deep breath; it's about taking a relaxed breath.

A relaxed breath moves from the floor of your pelvis to the base of your neck—front, side and back. Your whole trunk moves as a wave of expansion, starting in your belly, moving through your diaphragm, then up to your chest. Then, like a wave, it naturally recedes back down as you exhale.

Some people claim that to take a deep breath, you need to expand your chest. Other will tell you to belly breathe. They are both wrong and right—you naturally breathe more in your chest when you are exerting yourself. But your belly moves more when you are relaxed—as in meditation or sleep. Don't worry about breathing more when you are exercising. Your body will naturally use its ability to expand and relax to its fullest. To increase that range and your "vital capacity," or your ability to exchange oxygen, you need to have a relaxed chest.

What many people don't know is that the *back* of your chest is also meant to move with each breath. Your ribs extend around your back. They certainly move less than in the front of your chest, but they should move. Your upper back will never get tight if they are moving. I have yoga teachers as clients who were never taught to move their backs with their ribs. When they did they were amazed at the increased depth of their breath.

That gets you to the belly breath that's taught in yoga and meditation. When your belly is the dominant area moving, you are more in the parasympathetic state of your autonomic nervous system, or that relaxed, idle state. (This is the state that is designed to bring back into balance the fight-or-flight response after you have escaped from the woolly mammoth.) That said, you shouldn't be breathing from that place all the time. You want to use your whole trunk.

To get there you will need to learn to relax your breath, your body, and your mind. Using the belly breath will help you get there.

The belly breath was the formal part of the Mindfulness-Based Stress Reduction Program. The success of the program occurred when students learned the informal part—breathing a full breath all the time. Breathing a relaxed, full breath is directly linked to being present and mindful. The converse, a limited breath, is linked to the stress response.

When you breathe fully and relaxed, you can't be stressed. Learning the relaxed breath when you're not stressed is the key. Gradually you start breathing fully in normal situations when you aren't thinking of breathing. Eventually you start breathing relaxed under stress. And when you're not breathing correctly, you notice. When you breathe as stress is occurring, stress goes through you. You don't store it in your body or mind—you are releasing it with your breath.

Sounds great, doesn't it? So why don't we just do it? The underlying reason is that to truly breathe is to truly feel and we're not used to it so we are afraid of it. We all know anything new is scary until we've done it a few times. When you hold your breath, even subtlety or unconsciously, you are *holding*. Breathing is inextricably linked to feeling (taking in and then releasing) what is occurring in you and around you.

Learning to Breathe: The Formal Practice
I recommend you purchase the audio of the MBSR program. It will be the easiest way to learn. You will be listening to someone talk you through the process. (There are hundreds of books on focusing your awareness on your belly breath, but the MBSR audio program is a great place to start.)

Find a comfortable chair in a space that is not distracting. Wear loose clothing. Close your eyes. Take a few easy, normal breaths. Feel your body. Is there anything you need to adjust to be more comfortable? If so, do it. Settle in to being there. Your mind will be doing its thing, which is OK.

Begin to feel your belly move as you breathe. Feel how it moves against your shirt, your pants and the back of the chair. That's it! Feel your belly move. You are now doing a powerful form of stress reduction and meditation.

Start with at least five minutes a day. Get it up to twenty minutes a day. When my partner and I taught the class, we had our students doing forty-five minutes a day after seven weeks. At twenty or more minutes a day, you start to change your unconscious habits. Your physiology begins to change. You have a skill that will begin to generalize into the informal practice of your daily living.

As you will discover, you can try to stay focused, but your mind will distract you. Your tension or stress response will want you to tense back up or think about something rather than relax more. This is where the practice comes in. If you like, buy a few of the books on the topic. Go to the course to deepen your practice.

No matter how you practice, just practice! As with learning anything, you will have tough days and easy days. I guarantee you *can* learn it. We saw hundreds of tense men and women learn it, and watched it transform their lives.

Learning to Breathe: The Informal Practice

For some people, as powerful as the formal practice is, it can become an escape. I have seen men and women get good at meditating, but not take that skill set into their daily lives. Their practice is an escape. As escapes go, they don't get any healthier. But if you want to be more relaxed, more present and more effective in your life, you need to expand this skill into who you are being in your whole life.

This is the part I like. This is where the change really happens. When a man can be simultaneously mindful of his body, emotions, thoughts, *and* his environment, he is a powerful man. He is a Remarkable Man.

As you learn to focus on your belly in the formal practice, become aware of your body through the day. Specifically, notice where and when you tense up. Are you holding your belly? Or are you holding up shoulders? I train my clients to ask themselves "Where am I holding?" over and over again. If you are holding someplace, which is likely the case, releasing is powerful.

Let go of it. Now, where are you feeling tension or holding? Let go of that. You get the picture. Keep letting go of the next place. It gets subtler and subtler. As you keep doing this, several things happen. First you become more aware of not only your body, but of everything. You start feeling more. Like I mentioned above, that can be scary. But it's OK—breathe. Stay focused and present and accept what you're experiencing.

Let your body learn this new behavior: relaxation under stress. It's not an oxymoron. You can be relaxed as stress is occurring.

You are now letting go of past stress. A current event will activate the stress response or tension; old events, beliefs, and stress are associated with that response. As you let go in the present, you let go of a small part of the past. In eight weeks of the MBSR program, we saw people heal chronic illness, looking and feeling younger as they released past stress.

This peeling away of tension is what sets you up to hold space for yourself and others. Even when you are having a stress response, you aren't stopping it. Hear this: it's not about being so relaxed that you never have another stress response. It's about letting yourself have them. Only when you allow your body and your emotions to experience what is occurring will you be fully present and not in reaction mode. You will be more powerful, more creative, and more effective.

Doing it

Do the formal practice at least once a day. Start with five minutes. Work up to twenty or more minutes per day for at least six weeks. If you tell yourself that you don't have the time, get present to your current relationship to stress and what it's costing you. We heard "*no* time" *all* the time from our high–stressed super-achievers, but they always found the time. After a month, you couldn't take it from them if you tried!

As you are driving, watching TV, or in your more passive activities, start observing where you are tense and relaxed. After two weeks of that, start observing during more active activities, like speaking to people. After two weeks of that, start tracking where you're holding while in stressful situations.

Having a men's group is a great place to do all this. I taught the entire MBSR to my group. As usual, some men said they didn't have time. But everyone did it, and every man took their new behavior to their entire life. Ultimately men found themselves less at the mercy of the stress in their lives. You can enroll your entire family in this if you want. Many men found keeping a journal of their experiences helpful, much like a runner's log.

There is no reason why you can't do these practices. They're free, easy, simple, challenging, and you can do them on your own.

Connecting with your body

The previous breathing tasks set the foundation not only for your emotional growth, but for powerfully using your body. By developing your breathing, you're connecting to your body.

To enhance this connection, I suggest you put your body under stress and mindfully relax it. Deliberately stress your body. Exercise is an excellent way. I have seen men who learned to relax their bodies by working out hard and getting looser. First they learned to relax, then they were able to up their workout intensity while staying relaxed.

Lower your daily stress levels so you can focus on being aware, breathing, and relaxing. The obvious method is yoga. The best kind of yoga is slow yoga with an instructor who is more focused on relaxation than stretching will teach your body to relax. He or she needs to keep you focused on going slow, feeling, breathing, and releasing.

For most men the thought of this kind of yoga is not exciting. I know you don't want to go to a yoga class dressed in yoga clothes. But you don't need to wear yoga clothes. The right class will have other tight men in it. You won't feel embarrassed or too competitive.

Yoga is growing in popularity with men because it works, it's fun, and there are many secondary benefits (cute, fit women is one).

Another way to reconnect to your body is through bodywork. Acupuncture, therapeutic massage, and Rolfing® (SI) are three common ways. First, they all relax chronic tension. They also can teach you to let go and release when you feel discomfort. There is no better way to learn to relax your body than when someone is slowly leaning on your leg with the side of his or her arm. Your body's first response is to resist, to fight the intrusion. If the practitioner is going slow, your body will catch up and slowly relax. In that first instant of relaxation, you will feel about 10% more pain. Being willing to feel that extra pain allows the tissue and your body to release; if you do that a hundred times in a session, you will have deep relaxation.

When considering bodywork versus yoga, keep in mind that bodywork is completely passive. Because of that and because of the individual attention and the precision of the therapist, you will probably see quicker changes with bodywork than with yoga. Men will often go to a yoga class, become aware of how tight they are, and go get "remedial help" through bodywork. They will return to the yoga class as one of the more flexible men.

If you are committed to being that Remarkable Man, you must enroll your body in the process. You will never get there, and certainly will not sustain it, without your body being aligned and supportive. So do one of these activities at least once a week. No excuses. You can do a month of experimenting. Try a yoga class, then a massage, then a different yoga class, etc. Just do it!

Mindfully hold space
As you are developing your breath and your body connection, develop your presence. Get to the point where you can walk into a room and be fully there.

Use your ability to be aware and your breath to feel your body as you're relating to people. Deliberately find or create situations where performance is not the goal. Find places where you can focus on just being. Find places where you can fail without consequences. You want situations where feeling and behaving in new ways is acceptable. Often places where you don't know the people, and they don't know you, will give you the most freedom to be your new, Remarkable self.[4]

Walk into a place with the intent to experience what occurs in a richer, deeper manner. Your goal is not an external outcome. It is an internal outcome of increasing your awareness and relaxation skills under stress. Like with your body in the previous exercise, you want the stress to be at a level where you can calibrate your response.

As you are speaking to a person, watch and feel what your mind and body are doing or want to do. Feel the tension, then relax it. Hear the voices in your head, then thank them and release them. Feel the urges to engage or disengage, then hold off if you can to see what occurs. Feel the urge to perform, then relax and listen to the other person. Look people in the eye, feel the tension of doing that and release it.

After you do this a few times, others as well as yourself will notice a difference in how you show up. Both men and women will trust you more.

---

[4] Toast Masters is renowned as a safe place to practice and develop presence. My caution is that, in spite of their safety, their prescribed way of speaking might be limiting for some. In the end every man has his own way of being present.

Chapter 2:
If It Ain't Working, Let It Die

"I'm the one that's got to die when it's time for me to die, so let me live my life the way I want to."

—Jimi Hendrix

Let go of what's not working so you have space for what can work

If it's not you, if it doesn't serve you, if it doesn't help you be the man you want to be, *bury it.*

Easier said than done? Don't worry. In this chapter, you'll learn some tools and models that will guide you on this journey. You will need to surrender to what you have resisted. Let go of the past. Don't let it shape your behavior anymore. Let your past die; grieve it and move on.

It's holding you back, so let it go

You may not be an addict, but you probably have patterns of thinking and behaviors that don't serve you. You also need to be free of them, to "sober up" from those patterns. Use your newfound mindfulness skills to become more aware of these behaviors. Use your directness as a man to get honest with yourself about them. Use your friends, particularly sober male friends, to be honest with you.

I know a bullshitter when I meet one—because I was a big one, and still can be. One reason I formed my men's groups is so I have men to tell me when I am bullshitting, even if I'm just fooling myself. One great thing about men is that they will be direct, particularly when they are asked. It is liberating to be in a group where full expression is encouraged.

Discover a new ally

As men we are good at disconnecting or pushing away parts of ourselves. If we can't understand it, control it, or fix it, we deny it. And there is no aspect of ourselves we shun more than our Shadow.

Carl Jung began using the term "Shadow" to represent the parts of us that we hide because we feel they are bad. A Shadow is not bad. It is just like the Shadow you cast on a sunny day. It is behind you, traveling with you wherever you go. Whatever we weren't allowed to experience, complete. or understand as a kid, we often relegate to our Shadow. For example, if saying no to your father's bullying wasn't OK, you might have developed a coping behavior where you became a good little boy, and later a nice guy. Here your Shadow would be your anger around defending yourself. You might believe that being assertive is not right. Underneath that belief may be the feeling that asserting yourself will produce retribution.

Shadows bring limitations, but they also bring gifts. In this example you learned sensitivity and civility. As the deeper negative consequences of your Shadow are released, so are its deeper gifts. Rather than being nice because that is your only choice, your friendliness is not merely a survival skill, it's now heartfelt.

You give your Shadow too much power, in part, because others told you certain limiting beliefs about you—and you believed them. You were in a place at that time to believe them. After a while your Shadow also becomes like a computer virus corrupting other programs. What harms you is not that you have these "bad" Shadow aspects, it's that you believe them to be bad and you hide them. Then they own you.

A man's story

Charlie came to one of our groups after his second failed marriage. He wasn't surprised that it ended, as he said it should have ended a few years sooner. Even though Charlie didn't know how to break this pattern, he knew he needed to learn something he hadn't learned.

Coming from a large family Charlie learned to survive and to get the attention he needed by acting out. He was a small stocky man with a chest that looked like a steel barrel you could roll down a hill. His walk was big for a small man; his mannerisms were also big and expressive. Without any perceivable effort, Charlie was always entertaining with his stories, jokes, or BS.

The uninitiated would ask Charlie, how could your ex-wives not like you? You are always fun and generous. Any woman would love to have a husband like you. For many years he believed this too.

The despair of his last divorce created a crack in his shell of an act. If you listened, you could hear his grief leaking out in moments of his stories. You could hear doubt leaking out. He was on a threshold of cracking open the whole shell, more than even he realized.

We give all new men some space to ramble. Gradually we take them out of telling another story and into getting to what is behind the stories. Charlie was a great storyteller, so it was harder to keep him focused on his emotions.

Persistence eventually paid off. Charlie's voice started to crack. We let it crack a few times before a man asked a question to take him deeper. When the man asked, he hit the bull's eye. Charlie stopped in his tracks. It was as if someone asked him a question in a foreign language that he thought he didn't know, but some part of him did know what the question was asking.

You could feel Charlie had to make a conscious decision after he allowed the question to penetrate his defenses. Was he going to act like the question didn't cause a reaction? Or was he going to speak from the place of the reaction? In that moment the world stopped. Time and space went to another dimension.

Charlie dug deep for a new courage to answer the question. I don't recall the question or his answer; the shifting of his axis I will never forget. With real emotion, Charlie started speaking about parts of his marriage he'd never spoken of, even to himself. He described how, as a kid, he learned to distract in the face of his or others' uncertainty and emotions. The more he spoke, the more I saw a little boy.

The next week Charlie came back a younger man. He'd left behind the part of his Shadow that told him he was less of a man for having feelings and needs. In the subsequent weeks he began his journey of letting go of those feelings and beliefs that a "good man" needs to do anything, at all costs, to keep everyone up.

Charlie began to understand his two ex-wives' comments of his not being there. He would argue about how much time he spent with them and all the trips they took together. Now he could feel how he wasn't there. There was grief for all those missed opportunities, grief for all those times when he thought he was there but actually was just playing his role of entertainer. In spite of his effort to do the right thing, Charlie saw how his behavior was his worst enemy.

The unraveling of the layers of shame from not validating his own emotions and desires allowed Charlie to see how he did the best he could as kid—and as an adult. The harder he tried to fix the problem, the more he made it worse. He began to understand that he was not only trying to fix something, he was trying to fix it with tools that were breaking it worse.

With the help of the group, Charlie began to let go of the beliefs that he wasn't good enough, that having needs wasn't OK, and that his only value to others was his ability to make them laugh. After feeling his anger at his father for setting him up to be this way, he began to accept his father for doing the best job he could with what he was given. As Charlie accepted his father, he accepted himself.

He still has his humor; in fact, it's better. Today he's not using it as a distraction but as a way to support himself and others in their experience of what is occurring. His humor now makes it safe for others to feel and express.

Behind the limitations of every unconstructive Shadow aspect is a gift. For Charlie, it was the sensitivity of his humor defense becoming the compassion for what is difficult to speak. He learned to accept and connect to what he pushed away. His Shadow behavior of being the entertainer who was always on, and rarely present, was accepted for what it really was. Charlie recognized that, in doing the best job of surviving his childhood he could, his friendliness kept him disconnected from his own experience and from others.

The Projector

Owning your Shadow's aspects allows you to own your projections. Those feelings and thoughts you're not aware of actually do go somewhere; they either go into your body as tension or out to others as projections.

What's a "projection"? It's when you're feeling something but won't acknowledge it, and you blame someone or attack someone else for expressing exactly the emotion you are trying to repress. For instance, when I'm not aware I'm angry or won't admit it, I am likely to find or create a situation where anger is present. My conscious mind gets to say, "It's them, not me!" and I convince myself that it's true. I momentarily experience an easing of tension by projecting my anger onto someone else, but I don't experience a release from the cause.

"The psychological rule says that when an inner situation is not made conscious, it happens outside as fate. That is to say, when the individual remains undivided and does not become conscious of his inner opposite, the world must perforce [helplessly] act out the conflict and be torn into opposing halves."

—Carl Jung, MD[5]

The development of your Shadow was your coping mechanism—a way to deal with a bad situation when you had limited resources. As a child you had no power. You were physically and emotionally dependent on adults who, for whatever reasons, may not have always put your best interests first. You had to do *something*. One thing you did, and probably wisely, was to hide your feelings and thoughts in your Shadow.

Until these energies are set free, they rule you in a subtle way. Often when you are "acting like a man," you are behaving out of some Shadow place. You are playing the role of being a man, rather than allowing your experience to be authentically expressed. This role could easily be a role taught to you or modeled for you. Every boy starts experiencing and expressing life authentically. He loses it when his environment for authenticity shrinks, when the space for full, genuine experiencing and expressing will not allow for his innocence. "Big boys don't cry," "suck it up," "crying is for babies." Remember all that? Those messages ate away at your safe place to feel.

In that shrunken environment, you had to adapt. Unconsciously, you searched for the best set of adaptive behaviors. Where better to look than to the adults around you

---

[5] Jung, C., Collected Works of C. G. Jung, Vol. 6. 2nd ed., Princeton University Press, 1971.

who were often playing roles *they* learned as children? You designed a unique character role that protected you, if not from physical injury, then at least from emotional pain.

In my men's groups, sometimes a man will come in with prior expense or a presence of being centered as a man. He'll speak his feelings and wants. He isn't shy to push other men to "do their work." Yet when his time comes to work, it becomes all about others. He might get louder and argumentative. He accuses men of making it about him. The senior men in the group know that he is in his role, projecting his feelings onto the group.

Owning your disowned parts, your Shadow, is a key to growing up and developing Masculine Emotional Intelligence. When you own those parts (that is, take responsibility for them) you will not project.

Note that I am *not* saying to *fix* those parts; I am saying you need to admit to yourself that those parts are part of you. Here is a signal: if you are overly agitated by a person or a situation, that's a sign that it's not just them. For example, if a man behaves as if he's a victim, and you feel an urgent need to give him your lecture on self–determination, you might be projecting. You slip into the teacher role to avoid identifying with him as a victim.

The cultural expectation is that men, when stressed, become domineering as our Shadows start to unconsciously rule us. Conversely, there are men who retreat when stressed because their Shadow is telling them they don't deserve to be stressed, that they're being too emotional. So they shut down.

Looking into the mirror

Another concept we use in our groups is the mirror. Another man is your mirror when in some way he or his behavior is similar to yours. His Shadow may be similar. As he gets mad, you get mad. Or as he checks out, you space out. Often in his early days with our group, the intensity of the communication activates many repressed emotions for a new man. I know that when I first started doing group work back in the 1970s, I was always stirred up. I came from a loving, but emotionally repressed, family. Being around people freely expressing their emotions brought up all my feelings from my Shadow about why that was wrong. It was very uncomfortable.

The intent with all this psychological talk is to help you get clear: how are you *not* being the man you want to be? You don't need to fully understand all these concepts, but you can begin to apply what you do understand to enhance your awareness of your subtle behaviors. In many situations you will need to do something different: speak your feelings. When you do, your Shadow, projections, and mirrors aren't driving the bus.

Break the projector, shatter the mirror

We undertake a process in our groups where each member in the group takes a turn sitting in the "hot seat" as each member shares with the man what he sees as his dark side, or Shadow. He might say, "I see in you my Shadow of ___." After the dark, we do a round on the light side with, "I see in you my gift of ___."

By speaking, hearing, and feeling what is hidden in your Shadow, you gain power over it. By expressing the projections and mirrors of the Shadow, what was "dark" loses it power over you. When you reveal what you hid you don't need to hide it any longer, even from yourself. It takes courage to hear and speak what is hidden. It is your willingness to be unreasonable, to not accept anything less than the truth that will make you the Remarkable Man you want to be.

If you don't have a group, you could start by making those two lists—dark and light—about yourself as you see yourself. It is safe to do that. It is liberating to let it out even if it is just to yourself on a piece of paper. Then, you could take the next courageous step and ask a few friends to do the same for you. They could be men or women. Have them write down the dark and light they see in you. This will take courage, *and* you will need to make it safe for them to do this. In other words, appreciate what it takes for them to do this. Do not argue with them when they give you this gift. Thank them. Just because they said it about you doesn't make it true. *They* might be projecting. It is your choice if you agree with what they see, but be gracious that they took the time to help you.

Just deal with it, you can do it

Again, it's not about alienating all your Shadow aspects; it's about allowing them to exist, as you would allow the existence of a shadow cast by the sun. Chill out about all this. I was as guilty about this as the next guy for taking all this too seriously. Think about it like learning a new sport—you *will* make mistakes. The more you forgive yourself for not being perfect, the easier and quicker you will achieve your goals.

Too many people make personal development a life-and-death situation. There are times when it will take what feels like a massive amount of focus and courage. The rest of the time, lighten up! There is a temptation to take on "men's work" as your new escape. I know I did. If you do, catch yourself, then go back to being yourself —as screwed up as you might be.

Bottom line, it's not about fixing, or about achieving perfection. It is about accepting yourself in order to be authentic. Being unreasonable means being the full mature expression of innocence. When you are Remarkable, you are fully yourself— including those Shadow parts.

Don't fear change—embrace it with Evolutionary Change

With change there is death. With death there is grief; but with death there is rebirth.

I created a five-stage process of transformation called Evolutionary Change. On my blog site, www.owenmarcus.com, I explain how deep change is instinctual and inevitable. You can fight the urge to change, and fight this innate change process, but resisting it only lengthens and deepens the suffering. As humans, we are damned and blessed with this urge to learn and grow. Like any trait, some have it stronger than others.

Joseph Campbell created his *Hero's Journey* as a framework in which to understand this growth. In his book *Hero with a Thousand Faces,* he used mythology and literature to describe the phases of this deep change.

As you travel through life, you are directed to release what is limiting you. Some people say Spirit is guiding this process. Others see it as a psychological phenomenon. Still others call it instinct or evolution. The "why" is inconsequential. We do it. Now it is time to understand the "how."

This process is interwoven into mythology, good literature and, of course, movies. George Lucas consulted with Campbell to make sure he got it right for his Star Wars movies. We are drawn to entertainment that incorporates these states of deep change because it's in all of us. You can say this is another form of projection (some therapists call it transference), but we vicariously experience the stages of transformation—or growing up—through the struggles of the characters in the book or on the screen. James Cameron's *Avatar* touched deeply that place in us that rejoices when we witness the deep change in another that we know is possible in us. As with classic mythology, the personal transformation in *Avatar* is linked to the transformation of society.

When you're being entertained, you learn unconsciously and deeply. Every culture has stories that teach their youth what it is to be an adult. These stories lay out an unconscious map of what you will experience as you grow up, planting seeds of thought for what it is to be an adult. Sometimes in our fast-paced culture, seeds are sown without clear, conscious intent—seeds based on values that we may or may not aspire to. Be aware of the path you're following. Make sure you're adhering to your values, not someone else's.

The core of my Evolutionary Change and Campbell's *Hero's Journey* is that you enter this journey to develop qualities that could not be learned any other way. Think back: where in your life have you learned the most powerful lessons? It wasn't sitting behind a school desk, was it? It was when you were in over your head. With the help of others (or maybe it seemed like luck), you did something you had never done before, and didn't know you could do, that miraculously got you out of the difficult situation.

This process can occur on a micro level or a macro level. It might be one short event or it could take place over years. Either way, it pushed you. You were forced to grow up. I know most of my growing up was initiated by unpleasant situations. But the catalytic, life-changing event could also be something like becoming a father, or having a business succeed beyond your expectations. As humans, it often takes pain to get us off our asses. Are you reading this book because you're in pain? Is something not working for you? Have all your old, fixed behaviors failed to get you where you want to be?

Here are the five steps of Evolutionary Change laid out in a simple manner:

1. Imagine
You begin to see you need to change because you want something new.

2. Commit
You begin the journey—there is no turning back.

3. Catalyze
You die and are reborn and with the help of others; the old, buried seed of your full potential germinates.

4. Manifest
The change begins to manifest what you need and desire.

5. Share
Anchor your change by sharing your new gift with others.

Through knowing that you are figuratively dying, the change process becomes more bearable. Studying this process will open you up to it more. You will surrender to it sooner and receive support sooner.

You can refuse to go on this journey, but the cost of doing so is that you will never fully grow to be the man you could be: that Remarkable Man. That call to action, to evolve, will not go away without a consequence. Unconsciously, you will create another similar opportunity for growth.

The unfortunate aspect of this scenario is that resisting it usually creates a situation that is even more difficult. A perfect example is the guy who keeps marrying the same kind of woman. You see it. You tell him, but he doesn't get it. Well, it can happen to you, too, if you don't kill what needs to die in you. It's more difficult to see it in yourself, but the phenomenon is the same.

Use this instinctual process to your benefit. Know that the chaos of your life might have a bigger purpose than just making it tough for you. Read mythology, read biographies of men you admire, watch movies that illustrate this ancestral transformation. The most powerful support comes from being with men who have traveled this path themselves. They can guide you, tell you that you're not crazy, and encourage you to hang in. More than anything, they will model the unreasonableness that is required to travel this journey of Evolutionary Change. Being with them will transmit something to you unconsciously that most of us didn't get as kids: an orientation in life toward remarkableness.

Growing is a process of death and rebirth. You see it in nature. The maple tree's leaves die every fall. Every spring the trees come back a little bigger, stronger, and more beautiful. Let what needs to die, die. Let go of what doesn't serve you. Reach down in yourself for those forgotten parts that are your pillar of strength. They are buried in the rubble of what has never served you.

A man's story

Many years ago, Brock came to me as a client. As so often happens, he thought his "problem" was one thing, only to discover it was something else entirely. Brock was one of those guys who was an athlete before he started walking. Sports were easy, fun, and always rewarding.

Brock's body made him a great deal of money and fame as an athletic gladiator. You can imagine what years of playing professional baseball would do to a body. His back was as tweaked as it could be and still function. It got to a point where any athletic endeavor would make him tighter and in more pain. Not playing was emotionally killing Brock, though; that pain was worse than his intense back pain.

His friends told him how I had helped them. Desperate, Brock was willing to try anything. He hobbled into my office with his large, strong body. Over several weeks, his back pain disappeared, revealing a more relaxed man. Through our sessions, Brock began speaking about his recent relationship that had ended. First, it was an occasional comment about what he and Patty would do. Then he would slip in a feeling or two. After a few more weeks of relaxing and building trust, he revealed how "Patty was the one."

With that admission the room fell silent. I could feel he wished he hadn't spoken those words. Not only was he feeling what was behind those words, he knew I would ask a question that would invite him to say more. I did.

For the next thirty minutes, Brock disclosed how, with Patty, he was more present then he had ever been with a woman, how he expressed in ways he didn't know possible. Once he spoke that statement, the plug to unexpressed emotions was removed. His voice cracked, his eyes watered and his breathing deepened. I just let him talk. I could tell he been needing to unload to someone for a while.

Being his witness deepened his trust in me. I could tell that, as much as he appreciated it, it scared his macho side to realize he'd opened up so much. In an indirect way, I told him how that was OK by sharing with him a little about a similar experience I had. I could tell that he relaxed because he wasn't the only one standing exposed.

Brock was a committed athlete, so I used his drive to excel at sports as the template for supporting his personal evolution. When I explained that it was not only OK that he still had these feelings for Patty, it was actually good, he became more receptive and revealed more beyond his relationship with Patty.

Between the Rolfing® (SI) relaxing his body and Brock letting go of unexpressed emotions, he started to deeply relax. He reported being exhausted, which fueled a need to exercise harder. I got him to agree to actually go the other way, knowing he would feel more tired. He backed off the relentless exercise. Brock embarked on a cycle of sleeping ten to fourteen hours a day. He wondered if he was depressed because he felt sad all the time, something he had never felt before in his life. Even with all the sleep he found himself more tired. He asked, "How could I be getting worse when I am doing less and sleeping more?"

I explained to him that all that exhaustion was from the tension from life, but particularly, in his case, from decades of intense physical training, often when his body was tired. I went on to explain the relationship among physical soft tissue pain, depression, and exhaustion. I told Brock how stress, even the "good stress" of playing the sports he loved, was stressful because there were times when his body wanted to rest and it couldn't. Being stressed, his body responded with an ongoing stress response, which is a survival response.

When his body experienced the survival stress response, it allocated all resources to survival. Over time, he wore down its reserves, his vital life force. He was so strong and healthy, it took decades before it manifested as a back problem. Compounded on the physical exhaustion was the emotional trauma of losing Patty.

When his body relaxed, he not only felt his old exhaustion, he also felt old grief he had never felt. There are many ways to explain what was occurring. His defenses were down, and his coping mechanism wasn't working. The constant tension that had kept him up and on was gone, so one release would be the set up for the next, and everything conspired to disassemble Brock's body, mind, and world as he knew it.

He was in the downward spiral of Evolutionary Change. He had some resistance, of course, but I have to say that Brock did surrender well. Having me tell him he wasn't nuts, and that others (including me) had survived this journey, helped him. He continued to share with me other experiences of loss in his life.

Brock saw me less and less regularly, but he checked in over the next year. Three months into it, Brock hit bottom. A man who was never scared was scared. He didn't know who he was or who he wanted to be. He had nothing to hold on to. His amazing body wasn't in pain, but it wasn't performing. He was sleeping. He was going through waves of deep grief. His career ended along with his "love of life." Brock was a man without a home.

After four months, everything shifted and all the exhaustion was gone. He moved through the depression and found a new place of contentment, with an inkling of a new purpose.

Look at it clearly, so you can kill it

In the previous step you learned about the importance of being present and how to create that experience on a day-to-day basis. With that deeper sense of being, I am now asking parts of you to die. Sometimes this process of death is the wake-up call for you to be present. Having something taken from you can force you to begin your journey, or help you begin the process of killing what is not you. Either way, something will die.

Your presence is required to allow for the learning and healing. Until you're present for the change, life's circumstances only repeat the opportunity again and again. Remember: growing up to be that Remarkable Man is not about fixing all the imperfections. It is about learning what you didn't get to learn. When you are present to all the parts of yourself, and the death of what you've outgrown, you start learning quickly and with grace and ease. Struggle can transform into adventure.

Accepting being a man means accepting the constant cycle of death and rebirth. The good news is this: it gets much easier. The hard work is letting go of the big blocks you picked up as a child. As you crack them and haul them off, you'll find yourself becoming better at removing what is in your way.

You need to let go of all that old trash to create space in your life. You can't bring what you want into your life if there's no room for it. As you'll see in your Evolutionary Change, in the middle of the process there is a moment when you have to decide to die. Then you step off the cliff, and fall to a sure death... to be free. On the way down, the fear may turn to grief or anger about lost opportunities. But as you fall farther, you start to feel like you're floating. Then, from out of nowhere, a large bird flies underneath you. He lifts you up, and then takes you to the other side.

After taking this leap of faith, it may feel as if you only stepped off a curb. But your soul will know you entered a death spiral that unwound your being so you could stand taller as a man.

Remarkable tasks
Exercises to learn, reinforce, and embody your growth as a Remarkable Man

Step into your Shadow
Once you stop running from your Shadow's perceived evils, you become a free man. So turn around and step into what you were unaware of, or afraid of, in the past.

Make a list of those parts of yourself of which you are ashamed. You know, those parts you don't want to admit to or want others to know about you. Do it over a few days, let it grow organically as you add examples of how you express these aspects. If you feel so inclined, draw it or paint it. The more ways you express them, the less they have you.

Once you have your list, invite trusted friends to add to it. Ask them to give you no more than three. In their zeal to help, they may become stirred up themselves and get carried away. It is not about being a perfectionist getting every last one. You never will. It's about owning the big ones so you can free up more energy. Again, they won't necessarily go away, but they will release their unconscious hold on you.

Next to each aspect, list what it did to you. Briefly name how it limited you or hurt you. Then name how it served or helped you. Give it your best shot. You adopted that particular belief or behavior as a survival skill; see how it helped you. The more you can accept the negative and positive qualities, the more you will see that Shadow aspect try to sneak back. This knowledge and acceptance will make you less vulnerable to your Shadow's pull.

Map out your Evolutionary Change
Deepen your understanding of Evolutionary Change. Go to my blog www.owenmarcus.com to learn more. If you are so inclined, read Joseph Campbell's book, *Hero with a Thousand Faces.* The more you live it and accept it, the more it becomes your ally. Appreciate that change can be initiated by you or it can find you. Either way, deep change will be the Evolutionary Change spiraling down and connecting you with disconnected aspects, hitting a bottom, then spiraling back up as you integrate and share your newfound connections and gifts.

The first step is to go back in your life and write a story, or tell a friend, about a time in your life when you experienced this magnitude of change. If you can't recall a time like that, choose a family member or close friend who experienced something that you witnessed. Look for a place where you or they entered an experience as one person and came out another.

Wake up this dormant part of yourself by delving also into forms of entertainment that illustrate Evolutionary Change. Watch less mindless TV and start watching shows and movies that are about men transforming themselves out of necessity or consequence. An excellent movie about the rites of passage as young men we all struggle with is *Green Street Hooligans*. After being thrown out of Harvard just before graduation, Matt, the main character, finds himself growing up with his London peers in ways he could not have at Harvard.

Green Street Hooligans is powerful in part because it's so entertaining. It's easy to relate to Matt. His emotions are real and intense. As with any Evolutionary Change journey, Matt's struggles forces him to let go of what is no longer him and risk going for something new.

The unconscious is powerful. If you stop feeding it junk and give it a map of deep change, you will change, and that change will be easier. A movie such as *Green Street Hooligans* will be a seed for that part of you to grow—even if you are fifty years old.

It's not too late to learn this. Watch a couple of these powerful stories every week. Within a few weeks you will start dreaming and thinking about the hero, that Remarkable Man in you.

Chapter 3: Leave Home —Really Leave Home— and Grow Up

"It doesn't matter what people tell you. It doesn't matter what they might say. Sometimes you have to leave home. Sometimes, running away means you're headed in the exact right direction."

—Alice Hoffman, *Practical Magic*

Leave the dependency on women

How can you possibly grow up if you're still living at home? I don't mean your parents' house, I don't mean your hometown. I mean, are you still living with the psychic and emotional bonds that keep you a child?

Indigenous cultures have ceremonies that mark the rites of passage from childhood to adulthood. In some of these ceremonies, the boy will be physically pulled away from the crying mother by the elder men of the tribe. It sounds cruel, but it's not meant to be. The mother is given the opportunity to outwardly mourn the loss of the son she brought into the world. The boy gets to see and feel that loss. His relationship to the feminine as he knew it—through his bond to his mother— is broken. Everyone gets to grieve. Without expressing their grief, they wouldn't have room for the next stage.

I never had a ceremony to mark my leaving home. I got a pat on my back and a "Good luck in college, son." Did you have a ceremony? Did you ever have an emotional conversation with either parent about how your past relationship as a boy was ending, and you were off to become a man?

Give it up

Regardless of what ritual of separation you and your parents observed, or didn't, you need to let go. It's not easy. Letting go means willingly giving up a part of yourself. Whenever you give away or lose a part of yourself, you'll feel grief. It might just be a passing feeling for a small item—it might be hard to give up your old baseball mitt, for instance. Or it can be years of mourning the loss of a loved one.

Remember step two? *If it no longer serves you, kill it.* Well, when something dies, there will be grief. Even if you feel your mother was a harridan from hell, she was still your mother. As a part of the grief, you may even be angry. Maybe you're still longing for some love, and giving up that longing, realizing you may never get what you want, makes you sad.

The act of letting go of what doesn't serve you is an act of courage. For a man, there is no more powerful relationship than the one with our mother. When we let go of its limitations we create space for a new relationship with the feminine.

A man's story

John came to me for chronic back pain. He was an accomplished trial attorney who could impress anyone with his verbal abilities; the man could recite long passages from great literature. But underneath his charm was anger that usually showed up as righteous control. He hated his father, who was very controlling and all-knowing. John never felt connected to him. Listening to John talk about his father, you'd think you were listening to a ten-year-old boy, not a 6'2"grown man in his forties. Interestingly, later in life, John's father had Parkinson's; two decades later, John developed Parkinson's.

I once heard a researcher speak about a fellow researcher whose wife was sick. After several tests she was found to have the very rare disease his friend was studying in his research lab. As the speaker pointed out, developing the disease was her way to get her husband's attention. Your unconscious is powerful. Unfelt and unexpressed feelings and needs will find a way to get what they want—even if it's not what *you* want. Did John develop Parkinson's as a way to connect with his father? Realistically, we'll never know for sure. But what do you think?

Observe your own behaviors as if you're a friend watching yourself. Go deeper than the obvious. As with the woman married to the scientist, often your behaviors will be an unconscious expression of what you feel and want that you aren't expressing, or even acknowledging, directly. Your incomplete break from home can manifest indirectly as emotional, relationship, or body issues. In spite of John's verbal abilities, he never had a real conversation with his father. He held his resentment in, only to have it manifest as an illness. Often, you won't know what you're holding in until you start to communicate. And you probably won't know the effect of holding it all in until you speak.

Unacknowledged and unexpressed feelings and needs from your childhood—and specifically towards your mother—will be projected onto your female partners. It's as if you keep repeating third grade until you learn those lessons. Your incompletion with your mother will be repeated in your struggle with your partners. Those stuck emotions develop into an unconscious straightjacket. You don't know anything different. You don't know what it would feel like *not* to have it on. Like a straightjacket, it even restricts your breath.

Saying that your failed romantic relationship has to do with your failed relationship with your mother may sound simplistic, but I am a firm believer that there are multiple causes for a problem. Some are primary causes. For many men I assisted, the shift in their relationships with women came from them making peace with their mothers.

A man's story

Tom joined the group in the middle of an ongoing crisis in his marriage. One week he was divorcing Cheryl, the next week they were going to work it out. After a year in the group, there was a little movement; their fights were less righteous crusades and more arguments. Yet Tom still struggled with doing the right thing—did he surrender to the reality of a failed marriage?

In the midst of this drama, his mother developed cancer. At first it looked like she would recover, but six months into the cancer it became obvious that she was dying. I remember the day Tom admitted to the group his mother would be dead in six months. Tom wailed uncontrollably as he felt his grief, then his shame about how he viewed his mother, then his anger about how she treated him, and then his grief about how he actually loved her.

For the next two months, Tom kept peeling away layer upon layer of denial and pain. At home he was doing the same thing. He started opening up to Cheryl about his mother. He hadn't been holding back before, he didn't even know these feelings were there. As a little boy, he learned to "check out" to survive the continual fights of his mother and father. Tom realized that whenever his mother had offered support, he had rejected it. He learned that receiving her support meant he would open up to her and express his feeling towards her. That was great— until the next fight between his parents where Tom felt torn. What should he do? Protect his mother, whom he loved and felt was being abused by his dad? Or should he take his father's side to maintain that relationship? He repeatedly chose a third option: to check out.

Through his work in the men's group and at home with Cheryl, he slowly learned to check back in and acknowledge those disconnected parts of himself. Often, each reconnection brought pain at first. With Tom's courage and persistence, he felt and expressed the pain, reaching a new place of acceptance.

All this was occurring as Tom reconnected directly with his mother through her dying process. They were able to have conversations they never had. Tom would spend a day at her house cleaning, cooking, and hanging out. As she got worse, he spent more and more time with her. Eventually, he became her caretaker, even washing her and placing her in her bed. It was beautiful to see how Tom was learning to love his mother again. The few times he was able to make it to the group during those months, he told us stories about being with his mother that had all of us in tears with his love.

The night Tom's mother died, he was there at the side of her bed, holding her hand, looking into her eyes, seeing a beautiful woman. He whispered into her ear that she could go. He was more than fine. He loved her and thanked her for all she had given him. As she exhaled her last breath, Tom let go of her hand, and he sat back to exhale too.

For more than forty years, Tom was holding his breath around his mother, then Cheryl. The mending of Tom and his mother's relationship released the demon that possessed him. Without any effort, Tom and Cheryl fell in love in a new way. The constant drama and arguments disappeared. Oh, they still have an occasional fight. But now they only last an hour or so before some new place of acceptance appears.

As with Tom, our mothers serve as our primary imprinting of the feminine. What she taught you consciously and unconsciously, along with your response, becomes the seed for other relationships with the feminine. You don't need to go back to heal every dark aspect of that relationship, but you do need to stop fighting it. To do that, you need to develop awareness, then acceptance. As you release yourself from your battle with your mother, I guarantee women will show up differently in your life. I know hundreds of men who are proof of how powerful this shift can be.

Take the woman out of you—but leave the feminine
Regardless of whether or not you appreciate the power of your unconscious, you still need to find your unique connection to the feminine.

A mature man isn't afraid of the feminine—or the masculine. But you will never discover your masculine side until you cut your energetic umbilical cord to the feminine. There are things that women aren't meant to provide to men or boys. It is critical that you stop looking to the feminine for those things. Maybe you grew out of being a mama's boy, yet you still look for getting all your emotional needs met by women. Or perhaps you can't be without a relationship with a woman for longer than a month.

Cutting your feminine umbilical cord is cutting your dependency on the feminine to be your sole source of emotional nourishment. Once out of the womb, we are continually growing to a place of independence.

In cutting this energetic cord to the feminine, you may feel fear, anger, sadness, and shame. Much of those feelings are the release of emotions repressed by your submission to the feminine, and from the void that is created by not having women to care for you.

Women continue to become more powerful in our society— and that's a good thing. Women who are powerful in their femininity are a gift to all of us. In juxtaposition to the feminine movement, the masculine movement has been much weaker. There are few men to model mature masculinity for us. Consequently, we often modeled ourselves after women.

As our fathers were working and doing their guy thing, our mothers were doing their New Woman thing as they took more and more power back. With the 50% divorce rate of this country, and women usually getting primary custody of the children, the disproportionate dominance of mothers in our lives further decreased masculine influence. Most of our teachers were women, too, deepening the void of a masculine presence. The lack of equal masculine presence for most boys in their homes and the predominance of women caregivers naturally lead boys to fill the void of masculine role models and support with feminine role models and support.

I commend all the women who stepped up, not just to be a woman, but also to fill the voids left by fathers not present— for whatever the reasons. The deep bond and commitment a mother has for her child inspires her to do things she never thought she could.

So how did you get along with these women? You learned to be nice. You learned to dial down your masculine nature. If you really mastered being nice, you became a wimp. You learned to sacrifice in order to survive. You did what you had to do.

Dr. Robert Glover, a psychotherapist and author of *No More Mr. Nice Guy,*[6] lays out the etiology of how men lost their power through being nice. As he points out, many nice guys did not have their needs met as boys. As a coping mechanism while they're attempting to get their needs met, they try to be nice. As men, Nice Guys apply the skills learned as boys in dealing with women. It doesn't work, so the Nice Guys try to be even nicer. Women will reject this niceness because they innately recognize it as inauthentic.

As Glover points out, when you make being nice your priority, you internalize a lack of self-worth. You develop a mask of niceness, hiding your true feelings and wants as you seek external approval. In your history of not getting your needs met, you created a strategy of appearing as if you have no needs—because if you have needs, you fear that you risk driving others away.

---

[6] Robert A. Glover, *No More Mr. Nice Guy!* (Running Press, 2003).

All this leads to giving to get. As kind as this might sound, it is still a manipulation others will sense on some level. Some part of them will not trust you, because you don't trust yourself. This need to caretake will often show up in bed. You will be 100% focused on pleasing her, not even aware of your experience and your body. Sure, your techniques might be good, but she'll know you're not really there. You become not much more to her than a big vibrator.

I know I sound harsh. But I've been there. I speak from painful personal experience. As one of these nice guys myself, I needed women and men to wake me up. I also needed role models and guidance on how to express my needs. Being a nice guy, you have a tendency to spin things to be positive. These days, I will gladly risk pissing a man off to have him experience the limitations of his niceness.

If you are one of these men, get real. Start speaking your feelings and needs. Put aside that childhood pattern of being seen and not heard. It will be difficult and awkward at first. Just keep doing it. Eventually your pseudo niceness will erode. That doesn't mean you'll automatically become an obnoxious jerk. It just means you'll be honest.

Next time you feel yourself wanting to do something for someone, just stop. Take a breath and get present. Feel what *you* really want. Beyond the urge to help, go deeper into what is behind that urge. I'm not saying to never help or be nice. I am just saying do it mindfully, not automatically or just because you're "supposed to." Be present with what you feel and want. On some occasions, your motivation will be genuine. Other times it will be clear you are in your nice guy pattern. Stop so you can experience the feeling that you haven't allowed yourself to feel. By experiencing, accepting, and releasing, you will know what to do next.

You may not want to proceed. You may not want to speak your need instead of jumping in and helping. I know that's scary, but it's hugely powerful. Speaking the unspeakable will set you free. It's not even about whether you get or don't get what you want. The empowerment comes from just saying your need out loud. As you speak those unspeakable feelings and wants, you will become a more powerful man. Others will trust you more.

Women will be more attracted to you because, as author and speaker David Deida says, you are creating polarity. Growing up modeling the feminine, men don't develop the male balance opposition. The converse energy of the feminine attracts the masculine, just as two opposite poles of magnets attract. I'm talking about this in a *healthy* way—not in the way a weak woman is attracted to a jerk who treats her like trash. A healthy, emotionally mature woman will instinctively feel the balance of your energy and hers, and feel more attracted to you.

A man's story

Pat was a man raised by women. He had a strong mother, four sisters, and a father who was not emotionally present. Pat's father was a Nice Guy. He worked hard, loved his kids, and did what his wife told him to do—not that he shouldn't listen to his wife. From an early age Pat learned empathy; he had to understand women if he was to survive. Like many boys he played sports and had other boys as friends. But he always came home to a house dominated by feminine energy. You might think that Pat would have rebelled against all that feminine. He didn't. Maybe because his mother was a loving mother and his sisters were kind to him.

Today Pat is a psychotherapist, and what better use of his empathy skills? Listening and understanding are two great skills Pat possesses. He can just be there for anyone. He is a

Nice Guy in all ways. Everyone likes Pat... well, almost everyone.

Soon after their wedding, Ann, Pat's wife, started to become more assertive, leaning toward angry. Little infractions, like forgetting to pick up a shirt at the cleaners, developed into a huge argument. After three kids and what evolved to be one ongoing argument, Pat knew he was trapped.

How can a Nice Guy get out of a mess like that? I don't know of a way, do you? He tried empathy, understanding that her childhood was tough. He tried reason... what woman can't understand reason? Yeah, right. Women don't base their relationship behavior on that. He tried long, late-night talks, all to no avail.

Pat was desperate, so he stepped out of his comfort zone and joined our group. He easily adjusted to it. During the meetings, he would interject insightful comments. When his turn came to work he would report on his life and how he was "working on it." After a few months of him telling us the same observations, we started asking deeper questions, such as, "What do you *feel* when your wife fights with you or criticizes you?"

Pat's first set of responses was to say he understood her, she was going through a tough time, I just listen, etc. But someone would invariably ask, "So, Pat what were *you* feeling?" Eventually he would admit he felt a "little angry." That answer would get a group member angry. The man would admit that he felt angry that Pat wasn't expressing his anger.

After decades of never being angry—certainly not around women—and being a trained as a therapist to put others' feelings before his, Pat stopped feeling any anger. He was truly a Nice Guy. He was beyond anger. "Anger never solved a problem," or "no good comes from anger" were some of Pat's retorts to being questioned about his anger. He might say, "I can understand why that would make you angry," but we would never hear, "I am angry."

Through our persistence for emotional honesty, and Pat watching other men get angry and their world not disintegrating, Pat started to admit to his anger. He started being "unreasonable." Then he started to admit to it with Ann. For more than a year, Ann and he had almost daily discussions about their relationship.

Gradually, in Pat's reporting of these discussions, we heard how he got mad. We believed him because now we heard it in his voice, and saw it in his face getting red. Pat was angry. We encouraged him to speak about his other feelings to us and to Ann —those feeling of sadness from not being fully present for so much of his life. The shame of not standing up for himself, then the fear for speaking his truth, were areas Pat spoke about. If Pat is anything, he is persistent. He kept showing up, taking more and more little courageous steps toward being his own man.

In our group, we support and encourage the man to do everything possible to renew his relationship. My hope is that showing up emotionally, owning the past, and committing to a new future with present behavior can transform a relationship. Pat agreed. He started speaking for the relationship once he got his voice. Unfortunately, as he now says, it was too late.

Pat now says if he'd showed up in the beginning as he did at the end, they would probably still be married. Maybe. Pat also got to see how much of Ann's anger was the anger he wasn't feeling or expressing. In any relationship, not only romantic, if a person is not owning or expressing his or her feeling the other person will act them out unconsciously. With children in the stereotypical dysfunctional family, one role often taken is the "black sheep" role where that child acts out the craziness everyone is experiencing.

Now in his relationships with women, Pat is present. He still treats women well—not because he should, but because that is who he is. The first time he said "no" to a woman and the woman came back more attracted to Pat, he was blown away. He was like a little kid telling us how his "no" was a turn-on for a woman!

Today Pat is a Remarkable Man. He is a woman magnet. As he became more masculine, his women got less masculine. They became more feminine. Pat is a good man. Now he not only knows it, he is embodying it. He feels and expresses his emotions, so he is sensitive as always yet now not as a feminine man, but as a masculine man. He taught himself the parts of Masculine Emotional Intelligence that he didn't get to learn in a family immersed in feminine energies.

He is not emotionally focused on the woman as much as he is on himself. Pat didn't need to learn to listen and be aware of the woman, as some men need to learn. Pat needed to learn to listen, be aware of, and express his own emotions. Once he did that, women started feeling safer with him. He reports he is a better therapist because of this transformation. It is obvious he is having more fun at work and with women.

The feminine in men that works

Healthy boundaries not only protect you from even subtle violation, they send a signal to others that you're strong, that you can be trusted. Women will test your boundaries, usually unconsciously, to see if you'll stand up to them. If you can't stand up to them, how can you protect them? They won't feel safe.

The paradox is, you want to be nice *and* you want to be strong. What do you do? You risk pissing her off to be true to yourself; but if she doesn't respect what you value, do you want her as your partner? That sounds hard, but let's get honest. In most cases, she'll come around in a more powerful and loving way. She deserves a strong man, and it serves everyone when you are being strong. It's not about protecting your self-worth, it's about providing and protecting those you love.

We unconsciously learned the feminine ways to be powerful. It was only natural. We needed to fill a void of not having strong masculine models, and our mothers and teachers were the ones available. The downside of relying on being sensitive as our only communication style was that we further repressed our masculine traits. More of our psyche was taken up by more feminine traits. As desirable as they are, they become a crutch when you can't stand on your own as a man.

Your unconscious—and possibly conscious—attachment to your mother not only prevents you from being the man you want to be, it prevents you from developing the autonomous feminine side of your being. Sensitivity, which we'll call a feminine quality for now, is linked to women and not men. Your *feminine* sensitivity, because you are a man, is more passive, more elusive than it would be for a woman. When you express your sensitivity in a masculine manner, you don't collapse in it. You feel it, and express it with the focus of a man.

This might look like crying as you speak your feeling and wants. You might be shaking with the energy of releasing old trauma as you take a stand for what's right for you. Remember, taking a stand and being sensitive are not an either/or. As men, we have a great ability to be emotional *and* get the job done.

A man's story

While I was practicing in Scottsdale, Arizona, a teacher named Albert came to me as a client. Albert wasn't effeminate; neither was he in any way macho. He did have wide hips like you'd see on a woman. He was a friendly guy, but Albert wanted more out of life. It wasn't going anywhere for him. Teaching was boring. He wanted to be a principal but couldn't seem to get the focus and movement to make it happen.

Albert's father was in the military, and he was often gone. When he was home, he asserted his control to make up for the times he wasn't around. Young Albert became closer and closer to his mother because she protected him from his father's control. He loved how his mother would mother him, and he grew to fear and hate his father.

You get the picture. Albert gravitated toward the nicer parent. You can't blame him. Unfortunately, Albert gave up his masculine focus and the perseverance of masculine energy. His hips were the embodiment of a man trapped in a woman's emotional development.

Through the course of ten sessions and six months of integration, Albert let go of thinking, feeling, and behaving like a woman. First, he felt the impotence of not being a man. He then felt the anger he held towards both his father and mother. Then he felt the sadness of what he missed as a child and as an adult from his disconnect with the masculine. After letting go of the past, his body transformed. He lost his hips. Over the next few years, he became focused and became a principal.

When you cut the cord to your mother and your "womanliness," you have space to be a man with the feminine qualities that a man needs. After extracting the woman out of you, you can stand as a man who is connected to the full range of qualities a man has the potential to possess. You have extracted the feminine that is not you and held those boundaries, which become the pillars others count on from a man.

"Create" the parents you didn't have

The term "re-parenting" comes from Transactional Analysis.[7] Once you release the trauma, pain, and beliefs of your childhood, you are available to be parented in a healthier manner, thereby truly becoming mature. Without the release of some of the past, so often all that you are doing is laying another compromised layer, albeit maybe an improved layer, over a dysfunctional core. Inevitably the unconscious will sabotage the new behaviors.

Once the past is the past, you'll start seeking some reprogramming on what it is to be a man. You'll want to fill in the gaps in your maturation from when you were growing up. You'll want to learn what you didn't get to learn; that is, you'll want to learn how to be a man from men.

Your first inclination will be to do it by using old behaviors and beliefs, but this is where the re-learning comes in. If you do try the old way, it either won't work like it used to or it won't feel good. It will be like putting on an old suit that doesn't fit, or is now out of style. Let go of that old behavior as you fully experience the emotions associated with it. Allow yourself to feel the hole the behavior or belief creates in its departure, without trying to rationalize it. Practice your mindfulness of acceptance.

---

[7] Transactional Analysis, generally known as TA, advocates an integrative approach of psychotherapy, including elements of psychoanalytic, humanist, and cognitive approaches. It was developed by Canadian-born American psychiatrist Eric Berne during the late 1950s.

With re-parenting, you are teaching yourself not to recreate your past. For many men, what finally gets them into men's work, or just their own work, is realizing that unless they change, their children—especially their sons—will turn out like them (or, if not like them, in reaction to who they have been). Without some honest work and growth, their dysfunction would become their children's inheritance.

What you have difficulty accepting in yourself, you will have difficulty accepting in your son. Unconsciously you will reject in him what you reject in yourself. You rebel in an attempt to covertly assert yourself, but that becomes his rebellion against your authority.

Dr. Alice Miller, a Swiss psychologist, wrote about how parents live their incomplete childhoods through their kids, perpetuating the lineage of children who don't fully experience childhood[8] You need to find completion with your childhood— if not for yourself, then for your kids. This doesn't mean you need therapy twice a week for ten years. It means following the suggestions in this book to deprogram yourself from your childhood trauma so that you can grow up and be the man you want to be for your kids: the father you didn't have, the father the children you love deserve.

As an adult, seek out what you didn't get as a kid. Give up looking to get it indirectly from your kids. Find ways to get it directly as a man. When I hear the statement, "I want my kids to have everything I didn't have," I hear love along with unfulfilled needs. Of course we want a better life for our kids. But taking your kids to every possible class, activity, and sport may be more about you than them.

---

[8] Miller, Alice. *The Drama of the Gifted Child: the search for the true self,* Revised edition. New York: BasicBooks, 1997.

Re-parenting is re-learning, or learning for the first time, what you didn't get to learn as a kid—either because it wasn't taught to you or because the stress of the moment was too great to learn. Once you pull the weeds from the soil and fertilize it, it's time to plant what you want to grow. Use this book, read good literature, watch inspiring biopics, or hang with Remarkable Men to seed your new soil.

In an expanded way this whole book is about re-parenting. I am not saying you are screwed up. I am saying you never got to learn what you needed to learn to be that Remarkable Man. To grow up, to grow your abundant Victory Garden[9] from the new seeds of this book and from other Remarkable Men is the path to Remarkableness and increased Masculine Emotional Intelligence.

Leave home... be alone

In your journey of finally growing up, you'll discover times when you need to escape, to be alone, to reconnect to yourself. You'll crave your own time and space. This need for space is not imaginary. Your alone time and space might be meditation, it might be a weekend in the mountains, or it might be a two-year trip around the world.

Some time and space allows you to connect with a deeper and quieter part of yourself—or it can be an escape from the reality that is closing in on you, pushing you to grow up. When you crave this time, you might have to ask yourself, are you renewing? Growing up? Or running away?

If in doubt, ask others. Talk to your partner—not for advice, per se, but ask for feedback. Often those open-ended requests

---

[9] Victory Gardens were personal or shared community gardens during World War I and World War II to reduce the pressure on the public food supply.

for feedback reveal hidden feelings and desires for both parties. These conversations will bring more intimacy along the way to discovering what effects your subtle feelings and behaviors are having. Ask your guy friends, particularly the ones who are mature. You know the guys I'm talking about— the men who other men respect, and who women respect, too. From listening and talking about what is true in the moment, without an agenda, you'll express what you were unaware that you were even feeling. You are more likely to find what you need within yourself.

There will be times in your life when you're at a turning point. In traveling through these portals you'll need to leave something behind, something will need to die. Some part of all death is experienced alone. The moment when you hit the "dark night of the soul," the center of the third phase, or the catalyst stage, of the Evolutionary Change, you will be alone. If you had times alone before that moment, your surrender will be much easier and your ascent out of it much quicker.

Alone time and space on a regular basis is important. A man's castle is often *not* his home. A home is his private space, that place he goes to be alone, to create or to hang with his friends—a place to renew.

When a man takes on a partner, and then a family, he gives up a part of himself for something bigger. He invites others into his space—an act of generosity and love. After a while, if a man feels closed in, claustrophobic, what he might feel as regret is not regret—I propose—but our instinctual need for space. Some men love having a one-hour commute each way to work, because it's their alone time. And the smartest wives I know understand and protect their husbands' "man caves" (as one wife I know calls it), whether it's a den or office in the house, a workshop, or a garage. Men need space of their own. Where I live, men have shops. Men escape to their shops to build, repair, and just hang. Yes, sometimes we "go to the shop" to escape expressing our emotions. Yet there is another lighter side to our need to escape.

We are the hunters of the hunter-gatherers. Our ancestors roamed, and we need to roam by ourselves and with other men. We need to go on our quests. Business travel was the assumed domain for much of this journeying. But even when it was just men on the road, it wasn't enough.

The past couple of decades of Harley Davidson's growth expresses men's need to be free. We spend thousands of dollars to put loud pieces of metal between our legs—in some ways to escape the other pleasure we put between our legs. Before Harleys, there were horses as the vehicle of escape.

At the TED Global 2009 conference, Sam Martin spoke about "manspaces." His need for space inspired him to put on a tool belt for the first time and build a studio. In his research, he found a universal need among men for their manspaces.[10] He also found that many were beautiful creations —much more than crude spaces with pinups on the walls. He discovered men whose spaces were works of art.

We need space and time away from what demands our attention and energy. Men need it differently than women. Our need for space is in our DNA. If we don't create it consciously, we will create it unconsciously—remember your dad yelling at you to get out of his garage/workshop/den? Mature men nowadays explain that "this is Dad's space, and you are only allowed in if I invite you."

---

[10] Martin, Sam. *ManSpace: A Primal Guide to Marking Your Territory* Newtown: Taunton, 2006.

There is life after leaving home

Leaving home means being OK with being alone. The more you are OK being with only your own presence, the happier you will be, and the more you will exude a radiance of personal power. At one point as a kid, you could just bliss out being by yourself, doing nothing. When you allow that to return, your home will always be with you. Once regained, no one will take that from you.

Your kids, women, and other men will respect the healthy self-reliance you embody. Letting go of what doesn't serve you and replacing it with what you didn't get to learn will empower you to be your own Remarkable Man. Developing your own unique relationship to your feminine qualities—a relationship anchored in the masculine—is life affirming.

As a kid I couldn't understand why "nice girls" were so attracted to the "bad boys." Now I realize that these boys, as bad as they were and as poorly as they treated their girlfriends, were masculine. They had a masculine quality that I didn't have. I was jealous; I just didn't know why.

As the old macho evolves to a new masculine, represented by the Remarkable Man, women and men are inspired. You can be masculine without being an asshole. You can be sensitive without being a wimp. You can be Remarkable.

Remarkable tasks
Exercises to learn, reinforce, and embody your growth as a Remarkable Man

Do a ceremony
Over the years I have guided men in creating their own ceremonies to mark their separation from their childhood. You can create your own ceremony as the culmination of your journey of letting go. The ceremony educates your

subconscious that you are in a new place. It marks the passage. You have an actual physical memory of letting go.

Collect at least one small item that represents you as your mother's son. It might be a picture of you as a child, or even those "tidy whities" underwear (white briefs) that your mother bought for you and you keep buying for yourself. Take that picture, and any other tokens of your childhood that feel appropriate, to a quiet place in nature. Using the traditions of my teachers, as well as many Native American traditions, I will lay out a simple ending ceremony.

First, set your space. Find a physical location that feels good to you. It could be in the trees, in a meadow, by a stream, or by a large boulder. The point is that you feel good there. Create an imaginary line of intent around your space.

Do an invocation, a calling in of your Spirits or God. For some people, this is just a prayer asking for help and blessing for what you are about to do. For others, it might be calling in all Four Directions.[11] Use your invocation as a way to ground yourself in the present.

As you sit in your spot, connect up to the memories, bad and good, that you have of being a child. Then begin to focus on the memories with your mother in particular (or your father, if that's the focus of your ceremony[12]). Remember the ways she

---

[11] Simply, East is the fire, masculine Spirit; South is plant, water, emotions; West is earth, feminine, your body, death, and change; North is air, animals, and your mind, and the Center is your sexuality and life forces. You can find more detailed information online.

[12] If you need a ceremony to break an unhealthy connection with your father, you can use this same ceremony. Maybe your old baseball glove is the item, or a picture of you playing a game with your father. The rest of the ceremony would be the same.

was and wasn't there for you. Feel the closeness. Feel it in your body. Allow your feelings to come up. The rocks and trees are not going to care if you cry, yell, swear, or get crazy. Let 'er rip.

As the feelings subside, take the token(s) out. See them as the embodiment of your bond with Mom. Imagine a contract you had with your mother to be her little boy. Then imagine canceling the contract, tearing it up and burning it. Once you have done that with your "contract," do it literally with the photo or any item that is burnable. As you go through all this, let the energy and emotions continue to leave you. Once you have completed the breaking of your contract and the burning of your objects, bury them. Put back into Mother Earth what is hers. (Even if this ceremony is for your father, still bury it. The burning represents the masculine, but the burying is also a final symbolic break.)

In traditional ways Mother Earth is our ultimate mother. The woman who raised you certainly is your mother, yet energetically Mother Earth represents where we come from and will return to. By burying your objects, set the intention that you are giving away your past and your grief to the earth.

Beyond the spiritual meaning you place on this ceremony, it does have a psychological effect. Don't underestimate the power of these ceremonies on your unconscious. Many years ago a woman named Cathy came to me for chronic pain. While being "Rolfed®," Cathy became emotional about her mother dying when she was a child. Cathy was a well-adjusted mother herself with a good marriage. Yet some part of her was incomplete. I offered a safe place for her to speak about her experience of her mother dying. It brought up more tears as I learned she was not allowed to attend the funeral because, as a child, it was assumed that she "wouldn't understand."

In that moment I decided to create an impromptu imaginary funeral. This time she was there standing at the grave site watching her mother lowered into the ground. I had her say her last words to her mother, fully feeling and expressing her loss. We took the time she needed to have what she never got. Once she was done, I had her throw dirt on the casket. Then she watched the dirt shoveled over her mother. After her mother's "burial," Cathy was a different woman. Her chronic pain was gone. Others noticed she was more alive. She had a spark she couldn't remember having.

Ceremonies have power. Ceremonies are a way for you to reclaim your own power, rather than letting your childhood have power over you. You can adapt this format to release any part of you that is not working.

Balancing your feminine side
As you learned, as men we all have feminine aspects. The question is, are those aspects embodied in a masculine form? You won't know unless you look. So the first part of this exercise is to explore those hidden or unaware feminine parts of you.

I studied and limitedly practiced Ericksonian Hypnosis for years. Dr. Milton Erickson was a dyslexic psychiatrist who understood and used the unconscious mind better than anyone. The smallest suggestion when a person was not aware of it could make that person take a particular seat in a room, climb a certain mountain, or eat a particular food. Being dyslexic, Erickson was at an advantage when it came to understanding the unconscious. His conscious mind worked like others' unconscious minds. A normal conversation with the man was a trance induction, post-hypnotic suggestions and conscious reintegration all done in what seemed like a normal conversation.

I can tell you, from personal experience, that being tense is not a good defense to manipulation. Being present, in your body and conscious of your emotions is your best defense. When you are disconnected, you are already in a light trance, easily susceptible to another's induction or for that matter seduction (another topic of a different time).

Take your unconscious thoughts, feelings, and behaviors around your feminine nature and make them conscious through the following actions:

1. Your feminine and masculine list

    a. Write down what you consider masculine and feminine.
    b. Ask others what they consider masculine and feminine.
    c. Research these qualities on the Internet.
    d. Create your master list.
    e. Next to each quality, write how it shows up in you. Assume it does. Maybe it does so indirectly, covertly, or unconsciously. If you like, create a scale to measure your level of each.
    f. Ask someone else to comment on those aspects relative to you.
    g. For at least a week keep coming back to your list and your feminine and masculine qualities. You will start seeing how the unaware becomes aware, in yourself as well as others. Just like when you buy yourself a new car and you start seeing them on the road.

2. Pick the three strongest feminine qualities you don't admire.

    a. Explore why, how, when, and from whom you learned them. What was happening in your life at that time?
    b. Discover what need was not being filled, or what feeling couldn't be felt or expressed when this occurred.

   c. Feel that feeling or want in your body. Allow yourself to
       go back to that time in your life when all this occurred.
   d. Once there, allow the scenario to play out as you feel it
       physically and emotionally.
   e. Now go back to where it began and re-script it so it
       plays out in an empowering, masculine manner.

3. Pick the weakest masculine qualities that you want to strengthen in yourself.
   a. Follow the same above procedures as you did with the
       feminine qualities.

4. In your current relationship, start shifting out of the weak feminine into the strong feminine.
   a. Using your mindfulness, notice when you drift back into
       an old pattern or an old state of mindlessness.
   b. Once you notice it, step back, accept it, feel it, release it,
       and replace it with what you want.
   c. Have compassion. If you are really doing this you will
       screw up. Good. You are learning. You are learning what
       you didn't get to learn.
   d. If you have someone to share your losses and wins with,
       do it.

Creating your space

As men we often think we don't deserve, or others deserve
before us. That is one of our admirable qualities until it takes
us out of being present. I don't care how strong or innately
generous you are, at some point you will need a place to renew.
If you don't get that, your physical and psychological health is
at risk.

When I ran the Mindfulness-Based Stress Reduction program,
we would get CEOs, physicians, attorneys, and other busy
professionals as students. The first thing they would tell us is
they were busier than other people, and they needed an

exemption from the daily forty-five minutes of practice. We said no.

We all have reasons why we can't give ourselves the most precious gift: time and space. These professionals, usually men, would insist that they didn't have the time. I would tell them that, in that case, they couldn't take the course. I believe everyone eventually agreed to do the practicing. By the fifth week of the eight-week course, you couldn't take those forty-five minutes away from them. Not only was the practice significantly helping them, those newfound forty-five uninterrupted minutes per day were precious to them.

Your assignment, if you choose to accept it: take at least twenty minutes per day alone for three weeks. There is low-quality alone time, such as vegging out in front of your TV with a beer, and there is high-quality alone time, such as sitting mindfully focusing on your breath. If you don't want to meditate mindfully, go be alone in nature. Go for a walk, not a run. Preferably don't turn your time into a workout. The goal here is to slow down, connect up with yourself, and let go.

If you want to cheat, which is OK, get a massage. Even a gentle yoga class could count. Part of being alone is using that time to renew yourself. A yoga class might not be alone time, but it's renewing and you aren't relating to others in the class as much as you are relating to yourself.

So do this unreasonable act: be alone. If you get any resistance, tell your partner/children/co-workers you are doing an assignment. The Mindfulness-Based Stress Reduction program became a great excuse for the students to be alone. For many it was a huge unintended perk.

Chapter 4:
Ask For Help: Growing Up is a Community Effort

"It takes courage to grow up and become who you really are."

—E.E. Cummings

Who do you call at 2 a.m. when your world explodes?

In a boy's optimum development, after the *being present* phase when he has experienced and accepted himself, he begins to learn how to separate himself from what is not working (the *let it die* phase). With the support of his family and community, he leaves the home as a boy to begin building his home as a man (*leave home* phase). Now that he is "on his own," he needs to create his own community of support. To do that, he continues to let go of what doesn't serve him while requesting and receiving the support he needs.

Weapons of self-destruction

"Weapons of self-destruction," to borrow a phrase from Robin Williams, are all the ways you sabotage yourself. We all do it, without conscious awareness. Your coping mechanisms, those behaviors that got you through childhood, run on automatic, protecting you even when there's no threat. For example, you might become controlling and pushy when stressed, or retreat and shut down when pushed.

To get over all the crap that you're holding onto, to move past those destructive behaviors, you'll need to get help. Building your life is a constant process of letting go, then learning to move forward with the help of others.

A man's story

Ron is a man's man. He's self-made. He came from the other sides of the tracks in Chicago. He literally fought his way out of his neighborhood—when a judge told him it was the Marines or jail, he chose the Marines. In the Marines, he met a challenge he couldn't control—which allowed him to direct his energies to more productive endeavors: first school, then business.

Ron built up a successful chain of restaurants, then ran the business as a battlefield general runs a war: he demanded excellence at any cost. It worked; he became hugely successful financially and politically. He was well-respected, even feared. His employees knew what they had to do, and they did it well. The business continued to grow until he eventually sold it.

Along the way he danced with alcoholism and rage. Both contributed to his divorce, as did his not being present physically and emotionally. He did a good job of anticipating the next thing for his business, but when his marriage fell apart it was an ugly surprise.

The skill set that got him out of that bad neighborhood helped him create a successful business—but those same skills led to his divorce and deep depression. When he sold his business and had no marriage, he was lost. There was nothing left to fight for or about. When your opponent steps out of the ring, what do you do?

Ron began a journey of recovering his missing parts. He started with good therapy. He was smart enough to find a therapist who was as smart as he was, and not afraid of him. At first he got more depressed and exhausted as he surrendered to the old pain that had always lurked below the surface, and occasionally came up to sabotage a relationship. But he finally felt the rage that he'd had no place to express as a kid in an unhealthy home, in a dangerous neighborhood.

After a year of hard work, Ron began to see the light at the end of the tunnel. He started feeling human. He was able to start having meaningful relationships. Yet there were still some saboteurs hiding inside of him. At first they just seemed to be aberrations to his new state of well-being, but they kept coming up. They were affecting his second marriage. This time he didn't want to lose his marriage so he knew he needed help. He also knew it needed to be more than good therapy.

Being a smart man, he asked around for what others recommended, and got several suggestions. He chose to pursue two that kept coming up. The first was to get Rolfed. The Rolfing® (SI) released an enormous amount of old physical and emotional tension. Six months after his ten sessions, he felt twenty years younger, his chronic back pain was gone, and for the first time in his life, Ron knew what it felt like to be relaxed. What really impressed him, though, was how he could be more present with people. His need to push was all but gone.

But with his new body-mind awareness came another awareness: there were things missing in his life. Along with his relaxation, he felt a deep loneliness, a loneliness that had always been there, just buried under all the rage and tension.

He pursued the second recommendation people had made: check out men's work, particularly Mankind Project's *New Warrior Training Adventure.*[13] He went off to do their weekend training... and finally, he was ready to be with men without attempting to control them.

After the training, he found a men's group to join. To this day, Ron continues to attend his weekly men's group meeting. He still has bouts of his old feelings and behaviors, but now they're minor and less frequent. Most importantly, he is mindful of them. He no longer denies his fear or anger, so he's not expressing it sideways by lashing out. His journey is now the inspiration and guide for other men on their journey out of pain to maturity.

We all develop a successful survival strategy—successful in the sense that you are still alive, but limited in the sense that it didn't provide you with everything you wanted. As a child, you adopted the beliefs and behaviors that produced the least

---

[13] See www.mkp.org for more information.

amount of pain given your circumstances. You got so good at believing and doing it that you continue to do it. As an adult, you might still be operating with the same programs you learned as a kid. You have always done it that way, it's kept you alive, and, in some ways, your world is organized around these programs, so you don't question them.

Ron finally started to question his "programs," his survival behaviors, when they weren't giving him what he really wanted in life. What coping mechanisms are you not questioning? Stupid question, I know—it's like asking a man what he doesn't see. But take some time to think about it. Notice how you react in a stressful situation. Look at where in your life you aren't getting what you want. Then look at what you're doing. What needs to change?

Get over it

We all need help. The first step of any twelve-step program is: "I admit that I am powerless over [my addiction/my anger/my childhood/my fear], and that my life has become unmanageable." For us men, this can be the most difficult step. It's hard for men to say, "I'm powerless." The light side of that is our innate provider and protector instinct; the dark side is that never asking for help becomes an escape or avoidance technique.

Simply put, if you don't have the life you want, there *is* a solution: get help. Life is not a math problem that has a simple answer. If it were, we'd all have figured it out by now, and be living the life we want.

As men, we analyze problems, calculate the variables, quantify the resources, and evaluate the players. Our hope is that, if we get enough information and are smart enough, we can fix it. If we can't, we apply more force. But you will never get there using those strategies. I know. I spent decades trying.

You have to get out of your head. I know that to do that you need to feel safe. And to feel safe, you need some kind of model, a way to frame your journey. This book can be that model. Let this book help you. All you need to do is go deep inside yourself—probably much deeper than you can even imagine at this point. Apply the suggestions. Explore some of the other ways to change. You don't need to do it alone. In fact, you probably *can't* do it alone.

But there's a secret you'll find out once you start your journey: *other men are dying to help you!* For men who are already on this journey, not only do we get to reinforce our changes by helping you, we get to feel like our screw-ups can help you not make the same mistakes. Owning our pain set us free, and it's a beautiful thing to watch it set others free.

Every week in our men's group, men share or experience new parts of themselves. Invariably, another man will later report how it contributed to him moving forward. Men are mirrors for other men. For example, if a man talks about his fear around asking his boss for a raise, there is at least one other man who has a similar issue who also becomes stirred up. As the first man works through his issue, the other man vicariously does the same.

The first man asking for assistance was a gift to the second. Taking the risk of being the first person to bring up an issue can be even more healing than the work itself. For many men speaking the unspeakable frees them. As clumsy as it might feel, speaking the truth or asking for help can be a significant healing.

Ask for directions

We all laugh at the stereotype of men never asking for directions. True or not, we need help when we're lost. Going around in circles makes you dizzy. What if you ask for directions, and listen to them, before you start your journey?

Reading this book is a step towards manning up and getting help. Getting help is not a statement that you're bad or worthless; it's a statement that your well-being is worth the investment of energy and time. Stepping up to ask for help, and then receiving it, is incredibly healing. You might have previously mocked a man for asking for help, but didn't you in some way admire his courage, too?

Growing up is a team sport

As men we need camaraderie. Why do you think we love the brotherhood of battle or the fellowship of team competition? It's in our genes.

When men are honest with other men, it breeds more trust and honor. Also, our innate drive to compete works here, too. I have seen men subtly compete on the field of honesty. When one man nails his truth, it resonates with a cord of truth in another man. The second man is driven to speak his truth. Competing not to be left behind, and feeling supported by his fellow man to step up, the second man speaks.

Structure of support

In our men's group, we create a safe "container" that invites men to take risks. The outside world is kept at bay. The dynamics of a group are based on shared agreements that allow for each man to know what is expected of him. He learns that if a man violates those agreements, that man will be held accountable. He also learns that this group of men is a safe place where he can screw up. He can risk a new behavior and still be accepted. Each man knows that the other men, and the group itself, have his back. This is all possible because the group container is strong.

Having your own strong container helps. So how do you do it? You do it by using this book to map out your development. You do it by setting goals for that development. You do it by creating your own container, a life that allows for time to be by yourself, to get help, to be with other men, and to integrate all of this. You do it by strengthening your maturity.

You also do it by bringing other experiences and people into your life to stir up and support your change. You may do it by ending relationships, jobs, and leaving residences that drain you. You do it by being sober, honest with yourself, and by having others you respect give you feedback. You may find mentors or models that have what you want.

If you don't currently have a men's group, or just a group of reliable men friends, you will see something amazing happen: those men will just show up in your life. Guardian angels, guides, teachers, whatever you want to call them, they just appear when you need them. All the men I know, including myself, have had this experience. As you move along on your journey, you will draw to you men who can teach and support you. However you create your container, you will be creating a container that excludes what doesn't support your change and includes what does support it.

I know it sounds hard-ass to say that you will exclude others. It is hard-ass. And it's often hard to do. You have ties to others as they have to you. Think of it like multiple cords attaching you to others. Inevitably, when you begin to change, these cords begin to pull on you. Some of the people in your life will not want you to change. When you change, it's a negative mirror to them. In other words, your growing up threatens them; they realize they need to grow up too, but refuse to look at that possibility, let alone support you in your growth.

For some people, it feels easier and safer to knock you down while you're attempting to escape the dysfunction than to admit there is dysfunction and to let it go. Shooting the messenger of truth is an easy shot to take. There are usually others who will rally behind this archer, shooting their own dark arrows, or negative comments, at you for attempting to change. Feeling the anger and sadness of the betrayal of your friends and family is painful. You're left in a position of deciding to remain unhappy and unfulfilled... or to break free and risk being alone.

The strongest pull for most men is from their "family of origin" (parents, siblings, and sometimes grandparents, cousins, etc.). It is often the black sheep of the family who is the first to have enough balls to risk the family's wrath. He's used to acting out and screwing up. This time his actions are more than acts of defiance, though; now they're acts of self-love. It doesn't mean that you won't get angry when others try to corral you back into your pen. You will, and you should, be angry. It means that what you're doing is first for yourself.

Part of healing your family issues is simply giving yourself what you didn't get as a kid: a structure of support. You may have been sheltered, clothed, and fed, but your emotional being wasn't always nourished as needed. You need to be willing to feel the anger, fear, and sadness about not having the family you wanted. Regardless of your parents doing the best they could, you were emotionally hungry. Creating in your life what you need to grow is a brave act.

When you change, others around you change. So by being "selfish" and focusing on your own growth, you set a new model for your family and others. At first, others unconsciously think, "If he can do it, I can do it." It's not necessarily that you're immediately successful in carving out the life you want, but watching you break free inspires others to try.

Sometimes a parent brings a kid to me, wanting me to "fix" their child. But I tell them the problem isn't with their child, it's in the child's environment; that is, the problem is the parents. So I ask them to work with me first. In most cases that resolves the problem. There is nothing more powerful than a parent growing.

So what helps?

Now that you're willing to step up, to create the structure to support your development, now that you feel the value of asking for and receiving help, you might be asking one question: where's the help? In the back of this book, there is a list of resources—many of them free. Use them!

Before you get overwhelmed looking at the list, let me give you some suggestions. First, this is not a sprint. It's a marathon, so pace yourself. It's great that you want to grow. But remember it took you all these years to develop into who you are today, and it will take a little time to disassemble that world to create your new world.

There is a slow track and a fast track to change. The slow will be less expensive. It will feel safer. It will allow more time for integration. It will be less disruptive to you and your life. The fast track can be intense at certain moments. It's not for everyone. It demands a higher level of immediate commitment. It demands a deeper level of honesty sooner in the process. It certainly requires more outside help.

On the fast track, you'll have more options to release what's limiting you, along with more options for elements to teach you. In the past, I have taken on a few men who wanted to be guided down a fast track. When I do that, though, I demand a strong commitment, because it's a large investment on both our parts.

If you don't have a guide, don't panic. You'll do the same work, just slower. Again, use this book as your road map to get started, and when you're ready for help, start by addressing your issues with the five categories listed below. (And remember that teachers will almost certainly appear when you need them!)

These categories are based on a Native American Medicine Wheel, the wheel that lays out all the aspects of our life.

Spirit
Your relationship to your Creator

Emotions
How you feel and express yourself

Body
Your physical body and health from a holistic perspective

Mind
More than your intellect, this includes your beliefs, too

Sexual energy
Your sexuality, relationships, and creativity along with your vital energy, or, as the Oriental Medical doctors call it, *chi.*

Don't know where to start? Go back to Chapter 1—just *be.* Pick any of the above; let's start with Spirit. Just get quiet, and be present. See what emotions and thoughts come up—how do you feel about your Creator? That part of your life that is more than you? What kind of relationship do you have with him/her? You don't need to be religious or spiritual. I am speaking to the part of your life you don't control. Acknowledge and express the feelings you have around your

Creator. Many men find themselves de-programming themselves from the guilt and fear instilled in them in their childhood religion. Other men, raised with no spiritual traditions whatsoever, discover an entirely new relationship with the Divine. Or it might show up as a deeper appreciation for nature.

There's no *right* way to do this. Some men like to camp alone in the wilderness to reconnect with their spiritual connection. Some men find peace in a new relationship with their church, synagogue, or mosque. Some men enjoy the more mystical aspects of Eastern religions. It doesn't matter how you do it, just do it. Explore and rediscover your relationship with your Creator.

Now, do that with each of the five categories. Ask yourself how that category shows up in your life, then ask yourself how you *want* it to show up.

Your journey to being Remarkable

A mature man owns all aspects of himself. He sees his life as a *process* of mastery, where the journey is the goal. There is no finishing line where mastery exists. Mastering your life is how you travel that journey.

On your journey, you'll want to quit. We all do. If you have started and then taken a break, come back. You deserve this.

Also, know that the beginning is the hardest. It's like getting in shape when you haven't exercised in twenty years—it hurts. It takes commitment to stick with it.

Get help. Find, or create, your community for support. We need communities. For the last 2.5 million years, since the Paleolithic period, we lived in tribes. It wasn't until about ten thousand years ago that we left the tribe for the farm; two hundred years ago, we left the farm for the factory. Now we've left the factory for the computer. All along that lineage we moved further from tribes, and yet our genome is 99.9% the same. We are hardwired to need a tight community.

Micros, or micro-communities (men's groups), are not just great as places for healing. They serve as places supporting all the changes that we as humans experience in a life. They are there to witness who we are and celebrate our wins. They are there to console us in our losses. They mark our rites of passages into different phases of our life. They teach and mentor us. They assist us in manifesting our dreams. They are our community.

Man up and ask for what you need—even if you're just asking for one of those teachers to show up in your life. You might not always get what you ask for. But you are far less likely to get it if you don't ask. Let go of the old belief that men need to do it alone. You and your family are worth every bit of this investment.

Know that within you is a deep, instinctual part that knows how to change. It's that part I spoke about before in *Evolutionary Change*. It's the hero in Joseph Campbell's *Hero's Journey*. Let that part come forth. Let it guide you. Be a leader, start your journey, and invite other men to join. Maybe you'll form a new group if you can't find the local support you want. When I decided to start, I had to take a deep breath and be willing to lead new men's groups, even though I was thinking, "Who the hell do you think you are to lead others? You're still finding your way!"

Finally I realized that the fact I was still *trying* to find my way was one of the gifts I had to bring to my group. Let go of the old paradigm of needing to know. Create a group of mutual leadership and self-discovery. Model the fact that it takes a community to grow a man—be that first man. As author and entrepreneur Seth Godin would say: create your tribe.

Remarkable tasks
Exercises to learn, reinforce and embody your growth as a Remarkable Man

Who are your saboteurs?

Know your enemy. Learn how you stop yourself from being that Remarkable Man with a growing Masculine Emotional Intelligence. Not having any awareness of your coping mechanisms for survival makes you vulnerable to their control. Under stress, what do you do when it gets to be too much, or could get to be too much? Do you run and hide? Do you come out fighting?

Here's the bad news. You will never completely remove these behaviors—but you can become much more aware of them and their tricks. You can reduce their need to show themselves. You can reduce their strength. And you can find more productive ways to achieve the same goals these behaviors were achieving.

Those behaviors served a purpose: they allowed you to survive. If you didn't have this particular set of behaviors, you would have others. You can get to a place where it takes a lot more stress before they show up—and when they do, you'll still be in control.

Awareness is the most powerful tool, so make a list of your saboteurs. Write down all the ways you check out, run, fight, or essentially end up not being the man you want to be. Do the list over the course of a week, coming back to it every day. Then ask others you trust if they see ways you sabotage yourself. And keep breathing! Know that we all have this list. No list is worse than any other.

Once you have your list of these negative coping mechanisms, you can do lists for your parents and others you grew up with. I suspect you will see a pattern. The more you can understand, feel, and accept your behaviors, the less of a hold they have on you. To deepen your work, go beyond your mental awareness. Feel in your body where these saboteurs live. Travel back to the last powerful time you felt each one of them, and what it felt like emotionally and physically. Keep breathing and letting go. What were you saying to yourself? What emotions are you aware of, and where in your body do you feel them?

Use your mindfulness skills to observe, accept, and release the strong emotion, the charge, associated with each of your saboteurs. They aren't going to disappear completely, but they can leave the driver's seat to become your backseat driver. That way, when they start "trying to drive," you know who's grabbing at the wheel. You can thank them for their suggestions, telling them that if it gets bad enough you will use their suggestions, but until then you are going to do it differently. Each time you make that choice to do it differently, they become weaker, and you become stronger.

You are reducing your saboteurs' power in two ways: first by reducing the stress in you and your life, and then by reducing the pull of these behaviors. Using both of these approaches, I have seen men who were always reacting to life move toward being present and creating their lives. Continue to notice what causes these behaviors to manifest and the power these behaviors have with you. In the beginning, it may be overwhelming. As an old friend of mine says, "sometimes the alligators are just too much, and you need to drain the swamp." You are draining your swamp, hopefully before you have to.

Create your support team

You are not in this alone. Who is on your team? If you don't have one, create one.

A good support team comprises a wide range of supporters. As your advisory council, they mostly model, mentor, guide, suggest, give feedback, and are just there for you. It's not so much that you are looking to create a team of subcontractors to build you your house; you are creating a team to guide you in the design and construction of that house.

The clearer you are on where you're going, the easier and more effectively you will create and use your team. Having a good sense of your purpose (see Chapter 7) will give you the needed direction. You can start with your purpose, and then create the vision and its goals. Possibly all you need is guidance on getting out of a hole. That's fine. Whatever is next in your life, you can have others support you in achieving it.

To figure out where you want to go and how to get there:

- Lay out what you want, whether it's what you want to create in, or remove from, your life.

- As best as you can, think about what steps you need to take to get to where you want to go, and write them down. Don't worry about getting it right.

- Next to each step, write down what you need. Specifically, what do you need to know how to do? Who do you need to guide you?

- Going through your list, who in your current circle pops up in your mind as someone who can offer assistance— even if it's just as a role model for you? Don't labor over this. You are brainstorming what man, woman, or organization could help you. Get into action. This is not school, you don't need to have it all perfected before you can apply it. The sooner you get support, the sooner you relax, the sooner you get more ideas and you start moving forward.

NOTE: The actual execution of your plan will not look like what you laid out. That's good; it shouldn't. You want to get it out of your head on paper, tweak it, and start working it.

- As you get support, thank your supporter. If he is directing you where you want to go, continue with him. If he is not, thank him and move on. If you keep working with a person, that person will expect you to more or less follow his advice. If it doesn't feel right to follow his advice, stop working with him. Remember though that sometimes even though it might not look in the moment like you're going where you want to go, since you've never done this before, you might be on exactly the right track and you just don't know it.

- Imagine your dream team of virtual supporters. These could be your heroes, living or dead. Ask them what they would do. As strange as this might sound, many men have benefitted from having their "imaginary" team of advisors. I occasionally place a specific person I know, or know of, in my position relative to a task to see what he would do. Often he does something I wouldn't have thought of doing.

- A large part of the support we all need is emotional. We want to know we are doing well. Admit that you need that, and get it. Be willing to open up to men who you respect, and who, if need be, will be brutally honest. As much as you want to hear good things, it's better to get the bad news sooner.

- Your list will evolve as you continue to use it. The more you ask for help, the easier it gets. Also, be a support for others. You will learn a lot from helping another man.

Chapter 5:
Fill in the Blanks

"The truth will set you free. But not until it is finished with you."

— David Foster Wallace, *Infinite Jest*

Find what is undone and finish it

How many times have you said to yourself, "Just get over it! Quit dwelling on it!" For me, it's too many times to count.

Most of the time, we don't get over it. We just repress it or deny it, because "big boys don't cry." But getting over it is not really completing it.

When you complete an issue, it's done. It has no power over you. It's not coming back to bite you in the ass (even indirectly). How many times have you thought you were finished with an issue with your partner, only to have it rear its ugly head again when you least expected it? You may not say it, but you will probably think, "What the hell? I thought we dealt with this!"

It's back because the head thought it was done, but the body and emotions didn't complete the experience. Understanding it is not completing it. Let me say that again:

Understanding what you believe an issue is about is not the same as completing it.

Descartes was wrong; you don't exist just because you can think. Your rational mind is only part of what makes you human. Your emotions and body are two more key parts.

When your head understands it on a logical level, and tells you to sit down and shut up, just like a misbehaving kid, your emotions will rebel. Your unconscious mind is more powerful than your conscious mind, and your unconscious is connected to your emotions and body. Your unconscious is the part of you that dreams and acts out. Your unconscious becomes that misbehaving kid when it's repressed.

Ever had the experience of just *thinking* about something that pissed you off, and getting mad all over again? But you tell yourself to "just get over it!" right? Well, you may *want* to be over it, but you aren't over it until your unconscious says you are. When your body and emotions have no reaction to that situation/person/experience, you're really over it. You're complete when that issue can come up and you don't immediately go into reaction mode.

NOTE: I am not saying that you should have no feeling or no response. You still may experience some emotions. But when you're complete, you're just noticing your emotions pass through you as you relive the event. Maybe without knowing it, you are practicing the mindfulness of the first stage.

Deep change

To complete an experience, you need to forgive and accept. Sounds easy, and sometimes it is. The grace that comes from accepting your thoughts and feelings generally comes after working through what you were avoiding. You could say this is Mindfulness 2.0.

With basic Mindfulness you learn to accept what is present, what's right in front of you. To complete, you go looking for what is hidden, what's causing your reaction. Or, when that reaction comes up, you don't brush it aside. To be Remarkable you can't be in denial of large parts of you. It is one thing to not know about, or be affected by, a "hole" in your maturation; it is another thing to deliberately avoid it. It's like having a toothache where your dentist says you have a cavity. Either you treat it or it *will* get worse.

Your life, your maturation, is a continuous story, always being played out. Sometimes the story gets too intense. In those moments, your first, instinctive reaction is the fight-or-flight response.[14] But when you can't fight or run, you have a little-known backup response: freezing or playing dead. The deer that gets taken down by the mountain lion can no longer fight or run, so he'll go into shock and mimic death. When the mountain lion leaves to get her family, the deer comes out of its survival trance and runs away.

Survivors of physical and sexual abuse talk about going into something like a survival trance. Psychologists call it disassociation. Shamans describe it as your soul becoming fragmented. Whatever it is, you're unaware of it. The trauma is stored in your body, in particular in your fascia system.[15] When a similar event or stimulus occurs, your old trauma and feelings are woken up. It's like hitting a particular note and feeling the tuning fork vibrate. Your past starts to resonate in your present, and in your body.

We recognize this happening in other people better than we recognize it in ourselves. When you've seen a person lose it over something that seems trivial to you, it's that person's past coming back to haunt him. It's as if some spyware took over his operating system when that button got pushed.

A man's story

You wonder why John got so mad at Rick when it seemed like such a little thing. But it's not about Rick: John is unconsciously attempting to complete an incomplete previous event. Let's assume John was beaten by his father for speaking his mind. Maybe Rick spoke his mind about an issue that John cares

---

[14] The fight-or-flight part of the autonomic nervous system is your hardwiring for survival. It's also the system that produces the stress response.

[15] Fascia is the connective tissue that holds all the muscles and organs of your body. It's the white sheets you see when you pull the skin off a chicken. Scar tissue is fascia turned into gristle.

deeply about. It's not about the issue, though. It's not even about the emotions, really—whether Rick offended or outraged John with his position on the issue. It's about the physiology of John trying to do what he couldn't when his father beat him. As a kid, John couldn't react. He had to take it. John couldn't fight or run. He had to take the hits.

But now John can stand up for himself. John's body has been charged with the energy of the past *for years*. The energy that would have gone into fighting or running—and, consequently, releasing and completing—went into his body. He became a compressed spring waiting to be released. One day, Rick pushed that button, and *wham!* John exploded. He might have limited himself to screaming and yelling, he might have escalated to physical violence... or, he might have run away, exercising his flight response. Either way, he still hasn't completed the experience. As long as John remains incomplete when it comes to feeling safe to speak his mind, he will continue to overreact to comments like Rick's.

The psychological interpretations of these kinds of events don't usually complete the healing. We assume that if we know the hows of a behavior, we can avoid experiencing the whys, the emotions. John may learn to avoid situations where his position is challenged in order to avoid blowing up. But it's not that simple. I wish it were. To fully heal and complete, you need to change your body as much as your head. For John to get to a point where he can be around people challenging him and not go off, he doesn't necessarily need to first understand that he explodes because his father beat him; he needs to allow the physiology of the trauma to complete.

Too many men remain stuck in the past, at the mercy of their childhood reactions. They believe they dealt with an issue because *intellectually* they understand it. Understanding it, however, is different from forgiving yourself for your reactions or accepting your experience and releasing the physical charge.

Don't be lulled into believing that if you don't react like John, you don't have incomplete events in your unconscious and your body. After thirty years of working with thousands of clients, I can assure you that we are all haunted by the past. For most of us, we're not haunted by major traumas but a series of micro-traumas—which can be worse. When you know you had a major trauma, it might be easier to understand and accept your coping behaviors. When you come from a "good family," never saw combat, and had what would be considered a good life, how do you explain your tension and disassociations?

Deep completion

There's another option besides exploding in rage, running away, or playing dead: drain off that charge in a controlled manner. The Remarkable Tasks (exercises) of this book and the resources at the end of the book will help you do that.

If you don't want to be ruled by your past, you need to complete your physiology. Over the years, the cutting-edge work with Post Traumatic Stress Disorder (PTSD) has shown us a way to release that coiled spring of emotion in a controlled manner. This research has removed much of the psychological stigma around our irrational behaviors. It taught us that often it's not the psychology, but the physiology, that is the cause. You're not some screwed-up guy with deep psychological issues; you're just in your own PTSD trap— and you can escape from it. When you realize you did the best you could as a kid— and that it worked, because you're alive—it becomes easier to accept yourself.

In the Mindfulness Stress Reduction Program classes I taught, I'd explain that we often learned to adapt a repressed version of the fight-or-flight survival response as our default stress response. The key there is *learned*; because it's a learned behavior, it can be *unlearned*. It's simple—in theory. In practice, unlearning it requires commitment and courage.

Deep completion is not one finite place. It's a place where you can be fluid, where you can be in the present without the past taking over—whether that be in the form of a rage response (fight), an anxiety attack (flight), or just shutting down emotionally (freezing).

In this fluid, mindful space, you can complete what needs to be completed. Some people get there with a few intense experiences. But most people experience many micro-moments of accepting what is occurring.

When John realizes why Rick set him off, he can back up and deal with that one issue. In the moment, he can breathe, allowing himself to feel in some small way the pain and charge of the current moment and related past moments. In a PTSD moment, it's as if past moments and present moments collide. It's probably a safe bet that he has other issues with his father and his childhood, but you have to start somewhere, right?

Deep forgiveness

An interesting thing happens when you forgive. You gain respect. If you forgive yourself, you start respecting yourself more. If you forgive another, you build respect for him.

Forgiveness is a vital component of completing. Forgive yourself and others who may have hurt you. You need to own your part of the process.

NOTE: This is not to say that people didn't victimize you; an abusive parent certainly victimized you. But later, in your unconscious's attempt to help you complete the experience, you create similar events and relationships to complete that past pattern so that you can release its tension. Accept your part of creating that.

I am not saying you caused someone to victimize you. You did not "ask for it." When it happened, you did the best you could to survive. In your survival, you might have performed acts that you regret. For example, maybe your dad beat you. Now as an adult, you remember how you picked on your younger brother. I have seen men distraught with shame about how they picked on their younger brothers. Owning the fact that you did it is one thing; hanging yourself for it is another. As kids we "misbehaved" because we were not given other options. Accept that, as a child, you might have not been who you wanted to be.

A man's story

Several years ago, a good friend, Gary, betrayed me. It wasn't the first time a friend had betrayed me. I might be slow, but I'm not dumb: I saw a pattern, and the common denominator for the repetition of this pattern was me. I was determined to get to the other side of this issue. Using Gary as my mirror, I asked myself what I needed to have happen so I could forgive, trust, and maybe even respect Gary once again, knowing that forgiving Gary would help me accept and forgive myself. From asking myself how I could forgive Gary, I came up with a five-step process for forgiveness, outlined below.

It's vital to realize that this process is about *your* completions and healing. The belief that we should forgive our perpetrators is flawed and disempowering. You may never get to a place of forgiving the person who wronged you—and you don't need to. This process is about you getting an opportunity to feel, speak, and complete. The intent of the push to forgive people who have betrayed us is for us to recover the power that was taken by the situation.

Even if the person you want to forgive is not around, has passed away, or is unwilling to work this out with you, the energy or emotion from your relationship to that person is still in you. To shift that energy and complete the experience with that person, do the five steps as though you're talking to them. Imagine the person in front of you, and speak to them. You might write them a letter. Then, to the best of your abilities, put appropriate steps into action.

The way I lay this out requires a high level of ownership. I doubt you are going to see this from most people. I'm giving you this detail so you can apply it to your process of forgiving yourself, and owning your actions. When you can own your behavior, and admit to what you weren't saying with your words but with your actions, then you're going to shift that energy and see it move *fast*.

Growing up is greatly facilitated by taking the view that everything is up to you. Allow yourself to see your part in the dance. That allows you to take action to shift the patterns in yourself. Leave behind what doesn't work anymore and learn what works better.

First, do these five steps from the perspective of what you would need from your own "Gary," the perpetrator who wronged you, in order to forgive him (or her). If your perpetrator is not doing it with you, you may need to imagine the perpetrator telling you what you need to hear to help you complete it. Your perpetrator might never say he's sorry, but on some level, he feels it. Just tap into that, and imagine him saying what you need to hear. Then repeat the steps from the perspective of forgiving yourself for what happened.[16]

---

[16] This is not about "blaming the victim." Unfortunately, on some level, most children internalize negative situations and feel they are somehow to blame for what happened. Just be open to forgiving yourself, whether it's rational or not.

You can have a third person as a facilitator. Your perpetrator is guided by the facilitator so that you may just receive what is occurring. The facilitator needs to stick with the steps as laid out below. Ad-libbing or adding comments can create unneeded chaos.

The 5 Steps of Forgiveness
1. Admission

Look at specific ownership of what the person did. He needs to admit to the act and acknowledge its impact on you. It's one thing to say, "I lied to you;" it's another thing to say, "When I lied to you, I betrayed your trust in me. That betrayal left you angry and sad because you were counting on me to be there for you when you needed me, and I wasn't." You get the picture.

As he is speaking, you should be relaxing. If your gut is not letting go, he's not sincere. You still don't trust him. Tell him you don't. You will feel his authenticity or lack of it. Trust your feelings.

To help you understand what you need to feel, you are looking for him to take ownership of four behaviors. You want to hear and feel complete about his:

1. Thoughts
2. Actions
3. Feelings
4. Projections[17]

---

[17] Remember, a "projection" is when you're feeling something, but won't acknowledge it, and blame someone or attack someone else for expressing exactly the emotion you are trying to repress.

What was he thinking when he betrayed you? What specific actions did he do or not do? What covert or passive-aggressive actions did he take? This is a tricky one. He might have cracked a few jokes that weren't all that funny because they had a hidden edge to them. The jokes were him expressing his anger through "humor."

What were his feelings when he was betraying you? What part of him enjoyed doing it? Owning your dark side, that shadow behavior, is always powerful. When a man does that, everyone relaxes. It's as if the elephant in the room is finally named. It takes courage to reveal what you were hiding, and what was driving the immature behavior.

Once he owns his feelings, he can own his projections. Here he can address how he saw you betraying him. It might go deeper and he'll recognize how, his whole life, he's taken an offensive stance around betrayal; i.e., he knows others are going to betray him, so he betrays them first.

All this can lead to him owning his mirrors. He certainly doesn't need to use that term to express how you and this situation were a mirror of how he was treated by his father. He might talk about how his father was always promising to do things with him as a kid, but never doing them. He unconsciously saw you as his father.

2. Remorse

Remorse is more than an apology. It's feeling and expressing his pain for what he did. When a man is apologizing to you for what he did, are you feeling it? Is his apology just words, or is it heartfelt? Are you tensing or moving away from him? Or are you relaxing and opening up to him? Is he expressing what he doesn't want to feel? Is he owning and expressing in his apology what he was avoiding in betraying you?

This stage can be a continuation of the previous stage if the man was genuine in his emotions in the first stage. To go to the third stage he needs to get emotionally honest with you. He needs to own the impact of his actions, and he needs to feel them, too. You need to feel that he is feeling them.

Usually there are many layers. It might take a few minutes for him to warm up and open up. Rarely have I ever seen a man just go right to the heart of held emotions. Give the man space to get there. If he keeps spinning around the truth, tell him. He may be incapable or unwilling to get emotionally honest. He might need a trained facilitator to guide him. Don't tell him you forgive him when you don't.

3. Amends

Here he makes it right. Going beyond atonement, you are looking for actions that express the remorse of the previous stage. This is not punishment. It's letting him do something so that you both feel like the scale is level once again. Without some action you both risk losing the gains. The actions make it real to both of you. The actions also prove to you that he is committed to you and your relationship with him.

He needs to repay his debt to you. If he needs to repair the broken object, you might negotiate a way for it to happen. However it's done, you want to be complete at the end. It's possible you have some charge that needs to be expressed. You may need to state your wants and feelings for you to be complete. Do it. Let the past die at this stage. You both need to be done.

4. Changed behavior

Look for a history of changed behavior. I have seen men do a good job at moving though the three previous stages, only to revert back to their old behavior over time or under stress. For us men, honor is important. Honor is not acquired with words. It's earned with behavior over time.

If you're going to forgive the man and also trust and respect him, he needs to show integrity in his behavior. You will know if his behavior shows integrity if it's congruent with his words. This stage takes a while to anchor in place. Most men can talk the talk, but not every man walks the walk.

I have used this process in my coaching and groups with great success. It allows the person to disassemble their reaction into chunks they can understand, and then release.

5. Forgiveness

Once he has traveled through the four previous stages, you can forgive him without hesitation. You can now respect the man. You can now have a new, honest relationship with the man.

I have seen men travel this road with another man, and it is beautiful. When he reaches the fifth stage, the man who was originally angry, hurt, and untrusting now has deep love and respect for his friend. What is great about men is that we honor the work men do. When a man does it, we see it and respect it. I have been one of the men with tears running down his face when a man gets to this stage. I know how hard this journey can be, so when a man has the courage to stay the course to the end, I have deep respect for him.

Realize there may be some powerful breakthroughs, and that you will still want to see over time if the new behavior continues. If it doesn't, you have every right to withdraw your forgiveness, trust, and respect. Remember, you may not get to a place of lasting forgiveness, but you can have a huge breakthrough in going through the process. Gary never fully participated in my process; he certainly never significantly changed his behavior. I might not have full forgiveness and certainly don't have the trust and respect for him that I have for many men, but I do have compassion for his plight.

Every aspect of what I discussed can be applied personally. You can apply all the steps of this journey to forgiveness and to self-respect. You can request this of another person, you can offer it to a person you wronged, and you can do it with yourself. In all cases, have patience. Realize that this is a journey, and that it will take a while. You'll make mistakes along the way. Take the long view. See it as a deep healing that involves reprogramming old patterns.

Please remember, this process is ultimately about you, not the other person. It's not about getting the other person to do things, such as experiencing and expressing remorse. It's you doing what you need to do to feel complete so you can let go and forgive yourself, and possibly the other person. You may reach a point where you can forgive the perpetrator but not the act.

Going through this practice can allow you to regain your sense of power. As a victim it's hard to forgive another or yourself. As someone who took action and spoke, even if those behaviors didn't produce the desired result, you are much more capable of moving on from the situation.

Filling the holes of childhood

Do you ever feel like you're traveling through life, trying to figure out what you needed to learn, but didn't learn, as a kid? As much as our parents tried, and as much as you try as a parent, certain lessons will be left out or distorted. Many of your relationships are attempts to unconsciously learn what you missed. Knowing that can give you more compassion for others and yourself.

"She married her father." We've all heard that cliché. You're familiar with the concept that your partner *is* your parent. We have an innate need to complete our childhood with "good parents," so we use all our relationships as teaching tools. We're just trying to fill those holes left from our family and our childhood. We naturally seek to fill the gaps in our maturation.

You need to understand that you are re-parenting yourself.[18] It's important to get that, because it decreases the chance that you'll use something less than beneficial to fill those holes. If you understand that your mother was never available, maybe because she had to work, you will be more cautious about filling that need with the quickest or easiest solution. If you abhor being alone, you may settle for any relationship to fill your time and space. But that is not re-parenting; that is feeding the dragon of loneliness. In fact, you will probably have relationships with people who are either physically or emotionally unavailable.

Re-learning through that loneliness would mean *feeling* the loneliness. Allow yourself to truly, deeply experience that emotion. Feel the sadness. Acknowledge the hurt. That way when you have relationships, you won't settle for "junk food;" you'll go for the "whole foods" that really nourish you.

Completing your past to the best of your abilities on a psychological and physiological level allows for these holes to be filled with what will nourish you.

---

[18] See Chapter 3. The term "re-parenting" comes from Transactional Analysis, generally known as TA, which advocates an integrative approach to psychotherapy, including elements of psychoanalytic, humanist, and cognitive approaches. It was developed by Canadian-born American psychiatrist Eric Berne during the late 1950s.

Completing what is missing

Growing up is completing. It's not that you need to complete every incomplete aspect of your development, but you need to take on those big holes that you keep falling into. We all get good at stepping around the holes; maybe so good that we don't ever fall in. But what kind of life is that?

In Chapter 2 you learned about Evolutionary Change as an instinctual process every man has in him, and can use to make deep change happen. When you begin completing those larger holes in your development that you didn't get to complete (or didn't get to learn as a boy or a younger adult), you will often be traveling the journey of Evolutionary Change. That journey may call forth the need to undertake the Deep Forgiveness process, or Deep Forgiveness may put you on a journey of Evolutionary Change.

My experience with Gary set me on a journey of Evolutionary Change. It was as if every time I had ever been betrayed came up to complete itself. For a short period of time it was intense. I felt like the biggest victim on the planet. I felt very sorry for myself—then I was pissed. The Deep Forgiveness process evolved out of my Evolutionary Change. It was what I needed to complete and heal the pain "caused" by Gary, and to complete and heal the prior pain from similar experiences. If I was going to go through betrayal again, I wanted it to be good. And I wanted it to be the *last* time.

When you address an "emotional hole" by truly completing it, you plug a fissure that was draining your energy. Your life becomes a little more real and a little more honest as you complete these missing parts. Other men instinctively respect and trust you more. Women are drawn to you. You are safe while being present and powerful.

Women are dowsing rods for truth. More than other men, they will spot those gaps in your growth and your lack of maturity. They might not be able to articulate it, but they'll feel it. That is not to say you can't find a woman if you're a virtual field of maturity holes. It just means that the woman you find will have her own gaps in maturity. You can imagine what that can be like.

This is the fifth stage of nine. You're at the middle, the turning point. After this point it can start getting easier, particularly if you have truly embraced all the steps up to now. You have created a foundation of maturity. Congratulations!

Remarkable tasks
Exercises to learn, reinforce, and embody your growth as a Remarkable Man

Incompletion inventory
Get honest: what in your life haven't you completed that keeps coming up to bite you in the ass? Is it an old agreement with a friend? Or how you hurt a friend?

Create an ongoing list of items to complete. Prioritize the list. Start with the strongest, most difficult items. If that is too much, start with any item—just start.

As you fill these holes you will start feeling better about yourself. It's not much different from getting in shape—the first few runs are murderous, then it starts to get easier. The goal here is to stop losing energy. You might not fully understand what I mean by this until you complete one of these items. It's like getting a tooth fixed. You realize that you had gotten used to the pain, and once the pain is gone you remember what it's like to feel good.

Don't get obsessive about this. Maybe only one item really needs your attention. Many years ago I had to get honest. As a young man, I had two cases where I dishonored myself and others. The first time, I had an affair with my best friend's fiancée. The second time, I cheated on a woman before we completed our breakup. In both cases, I got my nerve up and confessed to the person I violated. It was hard to do, but I prided myself on being "a good man." To own up to people I cared about, to admit that I had dishonored them and our relationships, was hard. Both times, after I owned up, I had one of the best night's sleeps of my life.

Until I made these two calls I didn't know how much energy I was losing to things from my past. Where have you dishonored someone or yourself? Add it to your list. Make your calls, get clean.

Over the years I have helped men who had to get clean with a person who was dead. The procedure is the same, even though you will not get a response from the other.

The process:

1. Make your list of incomplete experiences, relationships, or actions. Who have you dishonored? What didn't you do or say that you should have?

2. Start taking action. Once a week choose one item to take on.

    a. As you complete, *breathe.* Stay as present as possible. Yes, it will make it more intense. But doing so will give you a bigger healing and more power.

b. Your action might be a phone call. Or it might be the entire Deep Forgiveness process. Don't shortchange yourself or the other person. If you are doing it, do it. Speak the unspeakable. Be unreasonable with your honesty. Invite the other person(s) to speak. The more you put into it, the more you will get out of it. The goal is to not only complete what is robbing your energy, but to complete in a way that won't cause you to repeat your mistake.

3. After each action, honor yourself.

a. You just did something few people ever do: you cleaned up your past without needing too. You did it on your own. That is being a Remarkable Man.

b. Give yourself a gift. Celebrate your courage, even if it didn't turn out as well as you hoped. You are not celebrating the results as much as your courage to take action. Turn the pain into pleasure. Leave the event with a good taste in your mouth. It will make achieving the next step easier.

Chapter 6:
Man Up! Take Responsibility
For Yourself!

"I am free, no matter what rules surround me. If I find them tolerable, I tolerate them; if I find them too obnoxious, I break them. I am free because I know that I alone am morally responsible for everything I do."

—Robert A. Heinlein

Develop the skills to live your life

Take responsibility for who you are and what you do. It's the core of what it is to be a man.

A responsible man is a man you can trust. He'll have your back. He's honorable. He's someone you respect. He's powerful.

A truly powerful man doesn't focus on controlling himself or others. He focuses on being responsible.

His realm of responsibility starts with his world first. He takes responsibility for his life, body, thoughts, and feelings. A responsible man is his own primary agent of change, not at the mercy of, or reacting to, others. He certainly will be affected by others and events, but he's not waiting for circumstance to shape his life. He is shaping it.

The space between being a control freak and a victim to your circumstances is the place of co-creation. To create, you need to first have a relationship with yourself. You need to respect who you are. You also need to have relationships with others you respect. With healthy relationships that support you, being responsible for creating the life you want is usually easier—and certainly much more fun.

Get your life back

To live a responsible life in relationship with others, you need to get back parts of yourself that you've given up. This whole book is about taking your life back. More specifically, you've almost certainly given up your responsibility in some aspects of your life. You need to take back that responsibility to be the man you want to be.

Your wife has the checkbook, so you have "no control" over your finances. Your boss is an ass who "won't let you get ahead." Your neighbor is a jerk who makes your life hell. Your kid is so disrespectful, you hate going home. Any of this sound familiar? Is there any place in your life where you're not happy, *but you're not doing anything to change it?*

While most of us have had these experiences at one time or another, if you find these and/or other negative experiences to be constant companions, maybe you are in the middle of the *Drama Triangle*. First described by Stephen Karpman, the Drama Triangle is a psychosocial model of how relationships go south. The drama is in the acting out of unconscious and covert behavior.

The melodrama occurs as the players, who are aspects of the triangle, start bouncing off each other. You need all three to have the play work. Sometimes, players will switch roles to keep the play going. The three roles are:

1. **Victim**, the person who is affected by circumstances or others

2. **Persecutor**, the person affecting or mistreating the victim

3. **Rescuer**, the person who intervenes to save the victim

Drama is good when it's entertainment; it's not good when you're in the middle of it in a relationship. It can be a trap. But you can shift your perspective, and your *behavior*, to get yourself out of this triangle. First, you need to understand what drives the limiting behaviors of all three players in the Drama Triangle and that the roles are malleable; that is to say, in the drama, we can all switch from one to the other depending on the moment and the circumstances.

Victim

A victim feels helpless and hopeless. He denies responsibility for his negative situation and denies having any power to change it. He often collapses emotionally and physically and feels as if he's in a no-win position.

He has no power. He can't say no. He can't take a stand. He feels violated, if only emotionally. Underneath the weak demeanor is the repressed anger from being violated. Because it is unexpressed, the anger shows up passive-aggressively through indirect, covert comments and actions. If he speaks directly, he risks more victimization, so the emotion comes out sideways, possibly as a wisecrack remark. But indirect expression never satiates the anger, so over time it builds as tension, frustration, and rage.

The victim also represses his grief for the loss of his power. Over time, these repressed feelings may lead to depression. He also has shame about being a victim, which only compounds his emotional repression. He may be the "Nice Guy" you read about in Chapter 3.

To shift this, he must begin asserting his feelings and preventing further violation. He needs to retrieve what was lost. The act of expressing is far more important than the results; he can ask for, but he may not get, what he wants. But through taking risks, and possibly not succeeding, he will begin to shift from being a victim to the creator of his world.

When he feels and expresses his sadness, rage, and hurt, he can begin to drain his huge lake of repressed emotion. He learns that loss doesn't need to be devastating. He can feel it, and then let it go. This allows him to release the fear of being victimized that is limiting his ability and power to create. If loss happens, he can accept the loss and move on.

The victim's emotional sensitivity can evolve into a unique gift. His innate empathy for other's pain not only makes others feel safe, it helps draw out their vulnerable emotions.

Persecutor

Every victim needs a persecutor. In the Drama Triangle, the bully is the persecutor who blames the victim, criticizes him or her, and sets the stage for the behavior of the rescuer.

It's easy to see the persecutor as a tyrant. His power is misplaced. He looks for a victim to pick on so he can feel his power and direct his repressed anger at someone. He may set up the victim to fail so he has a "dog to kick." But he is also a victim of this dysfunctional drama, and of his own misplaced power.

He—and others—can enjoy his power. When others are afraid to speak, act, or even move, just a little provoking can get a persecutor to take action. This man is often on the lookout for a good fight.

Buried under the bully is a victim. In my work with men who present as persecutors, they experience real healing by feeling and owning the part of themselves that was, and still feels he is, a victim. It can be difficult to see a man who has a large chest, a big presence, and overt power as a victim. Until he has a sense of this vulnerable part, though, he risks jumping back to his default coping mechanism of the persecutor.

This villain becomes the advocate when his abilities to speak and act are used in a positive manner. The courage to speak up can be used to challenge what is not right, in the personal realm, and even in the wider world. This power *can* be used for good.

Rescuer

The rescuer attempts to fix or change someone, rather than address his own emotions or needs. He fears the anger of the persecutor and the sadness of the victim. When the drama of this play starts to heat up, the rescuer needs to intervene to ameliorate the tension. This anxiety can become too much for him. So he'll constantly apply short-term solutions to a victim's problems while neglecting his own needs and feelings.

If he doesn't get pleasure, he at least receives covert power by taking away a victim's power to save himself. The victim is robbed of the opportunity to heal. The rescuer also robs the persecutor of his power to fully victimize. The rescuer hopes to be seen as a hero, saving the damsel in distress.

Beneath the desire to rescue is a desire and ability to facilitate healing. If the rescuer can refrain from rescuing, and intervene not to *save* the victim, but to assist when asked, he gets to help the person co-create a solution. In doing so, the victim is not further disempowered by being saved by another.

Get out of the drama

Awareness

First, know that you are in it. Change starts with accepting where you are. Admit you feel prey to a pattern. Feel your emotions. From there, breathe and relax to discover what is behind your behavior and those repressed feelings that you are not now fully experiencing.

Once you have gotten a sense of what is happening, begin to express your feelings. Take a risk. For example, if you find yourself being a victim, say no—go for what you want. If you are being a persecutor, feel your anger. What or who are you really angry with? If you can go deeper, what about the victim reminds you of yourself? If you are being the rescuer, what emotions are you trying to avoid?

What is the covert purpose?

What is your covert purpose in participating in this drama? That is, what are the secondary gains you get from perpetuating the drama? When you form a clear picture of your pattern, you won't get hooked by it the next time. For example, the passive-aggressive behavior of a victim is an indirect expression of assertiveness. Those biting, funny remarks give the joker a little power, don't they? But once the passive-aggressive behavior is owned, the drama stops. Only then can the clean, real power start to be expressed.

Speak the truth. It will set you free. The caveat is, however, that old patterns will die a slow death. If you have not spoken up for years, it will take several times for the other players to stop attempting to play the Drama Triangle with you. Your change of behavior will put these drama-based relationships at risk of ending. Others will attempt to hook you back in. Just don't go back into their play.

It is also possible that when you stop playing your role in the drama, others will feel the freedom of that and want to stop theirs as well. Be discerning of when they want to relate to you. Are they trying to hook you back in? Or are they genuinely interested in a new way of being with you?

When you become more aware of how you were benefitting from your covert behaviors, you'll clarify what you really need. The light of awareness will begin to shine on your deep purpose. You'll stop hiding from your dark side and start accepting your Shadow. You'll stop being a victim to your pattern of disempowerment.

Move to the center of the triangle

As you own your part in the triangle, you live less in its dysfunctional corners. In the center, you're in a place of balance. You can use the positive qualities of all the players without being played by them.

Under stress, you'll likely slip into one of the corners. But when you usually exist in the center, returning to a balanced place will be easy. Don't become rigid—it will take you out of the moment. Allow for mistakes and learning. You're not going for perfection; you want your newly-acquired skills of awareness, acceptance and courage to bring you back to the center. After a few times of screwing up and consciously coming back to center, you'll find that returning becomes natural.

As you develop your awareness and skills, you'll quickly spot the three players in other situations, without being in the play. With this new perspective, you will begin to shift to just watching it play out. Even with the old loop of the drama continually pulling you back, you'll feel more like a spectator of the play, rather than a cast member.

As an observer, you sit above the drama. You've moved out of the shame of being powerless to stop the drama to the power and clarity that comes from the acceptance of what was behind it. You hold a vision of something bigger that is empowering, loving, and life-affirming.

You are more than the rules

Are you a man of rules or principles? Principles are different from rules. Principles are alive; they're based on your core values, not someone else's guidelines. Rules often become arbitrary controllers. Are you hiding behind your rules or someone else's rules? Do you use rules as a means to escape being aware and self-responsible? Are rules your convenient excuses?

As men, we are excellent at using or manipulating rules for our personal benefits. Don't get me wrong, as a society we need laws. Still, it is interesting that in the United States almost three-quarters of the attorneys are men, and US attorneys make up 70% of the lawyers in the world. In an environment where we've made using and manipulating rules a national sport, it's difficult to address what's behind the rules we champion.

If you find yourself citing one rule after another, ask yourself: what are you protecting? What feeling or need are you hiding? Your ego might enjoy being smarter or quicker than the other man or a woman. But at the end of the day, are you happier that you won? The thing about winning arguments is, you may be right... but you're likely alone.

Often the man who argues his rules is a man trapped by those same rules. The cognitive dissonance[19] of needing to maintain consistency of behavior to match a belief system wears on you. It takes a lot of energy to maintain a set of rules and its belief system just to feel safe. It also alienates others.

Rules are often a coping mechanism for surviving childhood. Maybe your father was a rigid man with his set of rules. You learned his, then created your own set to survive. They worked. You survived. But are these rules in their latest version serving you? I suspect your set of rules is a cage containing your full expression and keeping out the full experience of the world.

---

[19] Cognitive dissonance is the stress of experiencing two opposing feelings or behaviors. People reduce cognitive dissonance by changing their attitudes, beliefs, and actions to match what is occurring. For example, if you buy an expensive car, you find reasons to justify the purchase.

Begin to notice when you start proclaiming a rule, even to yourself. What are you really feeling and wanting? You can keep advocating the rule, just be willing to also experience what's behind it. Loosen your cage just a little. If something slips out, good. You will learn that spontaneous expression is a good thing. Keep risking breaking your rules. Be that bad boy you want to be; live dangerously.

If you feel brave, push the envelope further. Start existing outside your box. Notice how many of the men you respect or admire are their own man. These men don't serve rules, they serve life. You can be one of those men.

Own your consequences

Boys to men

As boys, it was a game to see what we could get away with. We were respected by our friends when we weren't caught by successfully denying involvement in some mischief. As teenagers, we raised the bar on seeing what we could get away with. We were righteous about our freedom. But what we didn't consciously know was that we *wanted* limits.

As adolescents, we were learning to be men. We wanted to have all the freedom we perceived being a man was about, but we didn't want the responsibilities. And that's fine. That's what being an adolescent is about. We were learning in a controlled environment. It was the control part that we rebelled against, because that's what teenage boys do. It was also because we didn't want to admit to the adults that we needed limits. We needed them so much that we just kept pushing until we hit them. Remember the boys who had little parental control? Weren't they the ones most likely to be in trouble with the law?

As teenagers we were also going through our own rites of passage with our parents. In lieu of formal rites, our rebellion was our way of separating ourselves from the coddling of our parents. We demanded to be treated as men. In most cases, with no clear role models of what a mature man was, we ended up just imitating what a mature man would be if he were a teenager. Not the best plan.

A man's story

Rob came to one of our men's groups stuck. His life wasn't going anywhere. His marriage was deteriorating. His job sucked. He was feeling depressed.

Any man is welcome to experience the group as a guest. After five meetings, we ask you to decide if you want to be in the group, and then you need to commit to working. Being in the group meeting, even as an observer, will stir things up for you. All we ask is that you don't sit on it. You don't need to be proficient at expressing what's happening with you, you just need to be willing. The other core requirement is that you learn to take responsibility for your feelings, wants, and actions. Showing up and learning to be more responsible will change any man.

After five meetings, Rob said, "I'm in." He was good about showing up. Like most new members, he did more observing than participating, but when asked a question he would respond in a direct manner. Each week, Rob became more present, more alive. He reported that his wife noticed a difference in how he was relating to her.

About six months into his membership, Rob grew aloof. He subtlety withdrew, and his level of participation decreased. Each week, members commit to a "stretch," which is an agreement a man makes to himself and his group saying what he will do over the coming week. Rob started slipping on his stretches, not staying accountable for what he said he wanted to do. We all drop the ball sometimes, but when a man goes several weeks without picking it back up, we start asking why.

We asked Rob what was going on. He said, "Nothing." That was the red flag for the group.

Rob admitted he was back to his old level of drinking. He was bending the truth with his wife. He became passive-aggressive with us when we inquired what was going on for him. He made jokes about the group that had an edge to them. He likened us to being like his mother.

The senior men of the group immediately realized that we'd hit a wall. Rob's past had become present—but that's a good thing. When you reach that place, deep change occurs. In the face of an old pattern rearing its head, we have something to work with. We asked Rob if we could help him. He said yes.

We led Rob through one of our *Healing Journeys*, an intense process of going deep. Not only did Rob become aware of new aspects of himself, he had an emotional and physiological shift that was reflected in how his body changed. When the journey was done, we let him integrate his newfound wisdom for the rest of the night.

Rob came back the next week more present. Over the next few months we would dance back and forth with Rob showing up. A pattern began to emerge. Under pressure to perform, Rob would passively agree to perform, but then he'd only do the minimum, or nothing, if he could find a good excuse. When confronted, he got righteous about his position. He would argue that he technically did what he said he would. When that didn't work, he would deny all culpability.

Rob, with hostility, asked us who we thought we were. Were we trying to be his parents? For the men of the group it felt like a no-win situation. We liked Rob. We wanted to help him. We also wanted to hold him responsible to the group for his agreements. But when we took a stand with him, he pushed back, often covertly. Men in the group were getting frustrated. As the group spoke about their concerns and feelings of frustration with him, it was as if someone just removed the computer virus from Rob's brain. He got it. He began to see that he was still being a teenager, rebelling against his parents.

As it turned out, his parents talked a good talk, but they never actually held Rob accountable for his behaviors. Rob learned quickly how to play one divorced parent off the other. He got good at getting what he wanted. He made a life of manipulating situations and seducing people into getting what he wanted, or at least what he *thought* he wanted. But at the end of the day, Rob was alone.

His ownership of an old pattern was the shift he needed. Out of that meeting he began to grow up. He started to leave his teenager behind. His wife went from being repulsed by him to being attracted to him. His kids started listening to him and behaving. He eventually changed jobs to one that gave him energy instead of sucking his life force.

More men have arrested their development during their adolescence than any other part of the development. The freedom of being a teenager is seductive. Who wants to assume the responsibilities of being an adult? Modern society gives us many opportunities to remain teenagers with all the toys and distractions available. The lack of mature role models doesn't help. Why grow up when all the movie stars and pro athletes are having all the fun—and not facing any consequences?

What to own

So you want to grow up? Here are some areas to work on to be a mature man.

Start with your actions. You *are* your behaviors. They define you to the outside world. Of course, there's more to you than your behaviors, but your behaviors are your interactions with the world. Others know you through your behaviors. You can hide and deny for a while, but eventually, your actions will reveal your truth.

What are your actions telling people that you aren't saying aloud? What are the results of your actions? I always said and believed that I was an honest man. Yet my results were not supporting that statement. For many years I had employees, business associates, and professional colleagues betray me. I was resolute that it wasn't me—it was all those dishonest people.

As difficult as it was, I had to admit that I was the consistent person in these relationships. I was doing—or not doing—something that was causing a series of people to betray me. Eventually I got tired of being the victim. I began looking at what I did to create relationships that allowed people to betray me. I learned that the behavior I was *not* doing was pretty simple: I wasn't stating what I wanted, and taking a stand for it. I listened to what others said, and then I focused only on their words. I'd ignore or reject what I felt and saw. Their behaviors were telling me—even before I entered into a business relationship with them—that something was wrong. But I ignored the signals.

Gradually I learned to state what I felt and what I wanted. That behavior repelled some people but drew others closer. I started to notice the ones who were repelled were the ones I attracted in the past. I started to grow up. As a man, I took stances, not knowing if others would stand with me. It was scary. But I felt as if I had no choice. My past behavior was certainly not working. I didn't *want* to continue to put myself in relationships where I ended up betrayed.

Communications

For years I did not own the consequence of my lack of communication. I was talking the talk, but not walking the walk. I *said* that one should be open and honest, but I was unwilling to risk not being liked. Being liked was more important to me than my bottom-line. Because I was in the healthcare field, I felt I needed to speak and act in a "nice" way to my associates, as if they were my clients. Holding them accountable was not being a caring person. So again, I ignored the non-verbal signals. And I kept getting screwed!

In what way is your communication not supporting the outcome you want? Where are you saying one thing, and getting a different result than what you want or expect? If you're not clear on this, start asking people what they hear you saying. What are they feeling? What are they inspired to do from your communication?

Relationships

Are your relationships what you want? How do the people close to you reflect who you are? Do you make excuses for your friends? Again, what are your relationships saying about you that you aren't saying?

It was the quality of my business relationships that woke me up to my inconsistencies. I heard myself qualify who they were and the relationships I had with them. I was making excuses— so I had to look at what excuses I was making about myself, what excuses I was hiding behind.

Your relationships are mirrors for your relationship to yourself. For instance, if you don't learn from your first marriage, your next marriage will pick up where you left off in your development. With a relationship that's not working, *you have nothing to lose* if you try to turn it around. Dive into disassembling what isn't working. If the person doesn't want to help co-create a new relationship, you've got your message. If he or she does, get to work. Use the resources of this book to help you. See it as training. Speak your truth as best you can. You might lose the relationship, but you will gain valuable awareness and skills. And trust me—if you lose a relationship because you spoke your truth, it's not one you want to keep.

The willingness to risk a relationship for the truth is huge. It doesn't mean being bull-headed. It means speaking your truth at the risk of people not liking it and you. It means that you may lose the relationship. I don't know of a person who went through deep change who didn't experience a point when relationships were at risk of ending. Keeping your eyes on your prize—your vision of the man you want to be—will guide you through this. But it can be a lonely time.

A man's story

Henry came to our men's group as an outwardly emotionally healthy and successful man. At first, he thought he was looking for deeper friendships with men. His marriage was great, his kids were happy, his business was going well. Early on, he realized that, on some level, he was afraid to change. Things were good, so why screw it up? But as he spoke his truth more and more, and started feeling and expressing in ways he never had, there were some rough patches.

His father was a man who ruled with anger. Like many of us in those situations, Henry learned to be nice. His older sister got the brunt of his father's anger and disapproval, so Henry did everything he could to placate and please his father—just like his mother did. He learned from the feminine model: repress under a pleasant smile, not a cloud of anger.

Henry did an excellent job given the limitations of his learning environment. Once in the men's group, he started to improve upon his skills of emotional expression. He learned to express like a man. That sounds simple, and as a concept, it is. As a new behavior, however, it takes work over an extended period.

When you start to address what you think is not right, at some point, some relationships are put at risk. The relationship might not actually be at risk of ending, but for the man learning to be the man he wants to be, it can feel like he might lose the relationship.

As a child, Henry learned how to protect the feminine—at the cost of developing his masculine side. When he started speaking more from the emerging masculine side of himself, he equated that with not being a good man. You can understand how Henry would do that since his father's favorite form of expression was anger. Henry had to teach himself that male expression was more than just control and anger.

Henry began expressing from places he didn't know existed. Without effort he found himself being more powerful, and his marriage got even better. His kids were even happier. His business now runs even smoother; he's working with clients he really respects and who respect him. And, he certainly got what he had set out for in the first place: those rich, deep friendships with men. He also learned to love the little boy he once was, and respect the skills he developed to survive a difficult childhood. After a few years in the group, he is a leader and an example to the other men—and he's not yet forty.

Be an entrepreneur

Over the last thirty years, my clients have had every imaginable profession. My favorites are the entrepreneurs. These men and women are self-aware risk-takers. Starting and operating a business demands a lot of you. A business, more than any other endeavor, will force you to grow up, because you are the responsible person. There is no one else you can pass the buck to. It rests with you. Your success is often a reflection of your maturity. For instance, I've never met a successful business owner who was a victim.

An entrepreneur starts with a vision. He starts with something bigger than himself. He learns to serve that vision with his passion and his commitment. That vision, along with the efficacy of his business, attracts his employees, customers, and investors. He learns what he can accomplish, and then he uses all his faculties to take the needed risks. He's not fearless, necessarily; he just doesn't let fear stop him. But by taking those risks again and again, they get less scary. His fear decreases and his intuition improves. He views his mistakes as lessons on how to do it better next time.

You don't need to establish a business to receive the benefits of being an entrepreneur. Start approaching your life as a large business venture: What is your vision? What do you want from life? Have you written up your vision, mission and goals? Can you articulate who you are as a man? An entrepreneur has an elevator speech to describe his business; do you have a clear and concise statement of who you are as a man?

Recently in our men's group, we decided to distill our visions and missions down into taglines. Each man created a statement that affirmed who he was and who he was becoming. What is yours?

Look at where you want to invest your "resources" (not just your money, but your time and emotional energy). Get honest. You may need to discuss this with your partner. The more clarity and passion you bring, the more likely you are to get what you want. Don't get hung up on making it perfect, or even right. Don't let your fear stop you before you even start. Your vision is a work in progress. It will change.

Our unconscious minds are very powerful. They are always on. Even when we sleep, our unconscious works as it dreams.[20] As one of my teachers, Dr. Stephan Gilligan, taught me, if you don't have an affirming ritual or focus, your unconscious will default to a negative one. If you aren't clear about what you want, and have a way to focus on it, you will default to a lesser life. Take the time to explore what you want, then write it up. Create a personal "business plan."

Fear is an interesting emotion. In many ways, it's the opposite of anger. Anger is hot, explosive, and can be destructive to others. Fear is cold. It freezes and hides. Have you ever been so afraid that you shook? I have. Fear can stop you cold when you hit a threshold that you've never crossed before.

Entrepreneurs, like parents, have discovered that by having commitments bigger than yourself, it will often propel you across that threshold. The funny thing about us humans is that we often keep walking the edge of that threshold until something pushes us over. Having a commitment to a vision or to others pushes you through those fear thresholds. And the more you do it, the easier it gets.

That frozen panic melts when you do the act while feeling the fear. We are taught as men to grin and bear it. We are taught the way to get things done is to deny the fear. Don't let it control you. That might work in the short term. In the long term, it doesn't. The fear goes into your body, and makes the next time harder. It can also produce illnesses and sabotage you.

---

[20] *Indirect Hypnosis*, by Dr. Milton Erickson, MD

We teach the men in the men's groups to speak, shake, rage, cry, or do whatever they need to as they feel that fear. Just to fully experience it. At first, it's difficult. But as you keep doing it, the fear has less and less power over you as you truly feel it and experience it. When that experience is a part of you, you are its master. Instead of the energy drain it was, you now draw strength from the feeling of overcoming it.

Like an entrepreneur taking risks, you are allowing yourself to move forward with your fear in order to release old fear. Rather than adding to the fear through repression, you are releasing the old fear through acceptance. The enormous benefit of this is that *others* will grow to trust you more and more. Women will be drawn to you because you are safe. They will sense that fear doesn't stop you from being a man, so fear won't stop you from being accepting of them.

Because fear is less likely to stop them in their tracks, entrepreneurs are some of the best at taking a stand. They learn how to make decisions proactively, rather than as a reaction to a circumstance. Being proactive is no more risky than no action, and more likely to yield a positive result.

These men and women, in my experience, are far more likely to do the right thing, even when it might not serve them. There is something about having a business that makes you more responsible than you thought you could be. Not much different than being a parent and learning to grow up.

Entrepreneurs, much like athletes, learn that they will be tested. There will be times when they fail, when they make mistakes. They learn, and they move on. They also learn to prioritize their lives. Yes, sometimes they look back and regret some decisions. But the point here is that they took those risks in the first place.

Who are you?

Be honest with yourself about your feelings and needs. When you are not honest to the best of your abilities, your feelings and needs will come out sideways. Not only will that behavior sabotage you, it will turn off others, and they won't respect you. (Remember how I wasn't honest with my employees and business associates—and they kept screwing me over?) No one trusts a man who is not congruent with his word.

If you need some help figuring out who you are, and who you want to be, use these Five Aspects of Self to ask yourself a few questions. It will help you clarify your vision of the man you want to be.

Spirit
- Do you want a spiritual or religious connection?
- If so, how do you want to pursue it?

Emotions
- What emotions are floating around in your consciousness?
- What and who do you love?
- What are your unexpressed feelings and needs? And to whom do you need to express them?

Body
- What do you feel about your body?
- Do you like it? If not, why?
- What do you do for it?
- Do you have recurring pain anywhere? If so, how is it tied to emotion?

Mind
- How do you develop your mind? What are you feeding it? TV, news, and crap? Or things that fill you up?

Sexual energy

- Where is your sexual shame?
- How do you foster your creativity?
- Where is the emotional threshold in your primary relationship? That is, where does your relationship stop working or feeling good? Where do you get scared, stuck, or just fogged when you relate to you partner?
- If you don't have a relationship and want one, what are you doing about it?

These questions are meant to get you exploring what's hidden. Even the pinhole leak drains a balloon. The more you are aware of and surrender to your feelings and needs, the more energy, effectiveness, and power you will have.

Accountability

Hold yourself accountable so that you are the man you deserve to be. When you make a commitment to yourself or someone else, do you keep it? How important is your word? When you can't keep it, what do you do? Do you make excuses? Do you offer to make it right? Accountability is not about controlling yourself or someone else with shame; it's about being honest and real.

A responsible, mature man is accountable. Others count on him being true to his word. He goes through his life walking erect. He has no debts from his word. He does not lose energy because he has to be concerned about covering his ass. The Hindu *Bhagavad Gita* talks about karma being action. The Buddhists say there is only one right act, and that act is right for everyone. We all know the right act. When we don't do it, we become tense, we lose life force. When we do the right act, we gain energy.

We all have blind spots we slip over, even with the best of intentions. Through interaction with others we learn about these places within us. When you have people in your life who support you in your growth, in your journey to being more than you have been, they will give you the feedback you need. They will offer to support you in being accountable. Do you have people in your life to do this for you? Not as a way to show you where you're wrong, but as a way to teach you? Have you empowered these people to call you on your bullshit? Women are good at spotting it; men can be better at taking you through your dark areas.

There will be times when not keeping your word is the right thing; these are times when one commitment supersedes another. You might have promised your buddy to meet him for a beer after work, but you get a call that your son is sick and you need to pick him up, so you pick your son up instead. You are out of accountability because you didn't keep your word, but your integrity remains consistent with the man you want to be; obviously, picking up your sick child is more important than getting a beer with a friend. And hopefully, by now, you've attracted friends who respect that. So you don't make excuses; you make a decision and deal with the consequences.

Shift from *trying* to be accountable to just *being* it. Focusing on accountability for its own sake can limit you. Just be present with whatever task you're doing, and you'll naturally be accountable. I find we mess up when we aren't aware of our own experience. Stress will do this. You stop breathing. You get hyper-focused on the tasks at hand. Then you try to do more, so you multi-task, losing more focus. You lose the big picture.
Learn the awareness skills when you aren't stressed. Just like learning a sport, you do the drills off the field, so when you're in the game it's automatic.

While teaching Mindfulness Stress Reduction, we asked the students to take time to practice these skills. For the first couple of weeks of class, that was the biggest resistance for the students. But once they saw the benefits of being accountable, and learned to slow down, the forty-five minutes per day was precious to them. The skills they learned in their practice transferred quickly to the rest of their lives. They were less likely to make agreements they didn't want to keep, or that would be too difficult to keep.

Growing up and manning up

You grow up by learning and experiencing in new ways, and by learning new behaviors. Watch for the ways in which you aren't responsible, where your words don't match your actions. When you take responsibility for your life, and you become accountable for your words, actions, and intentions, then you are living as the man you want to be while having the Masculine Emotional Intelligence you deserve.

Remarkable tasks
Exercises to learn, reinforce, and embody your growth as a Remarkable Man

This is some of the most important work you can do. But, that said, it takes commitment to take on being fully responsible for your life.

Moving out of the Drama Triangle
Using what you learned about the Drama Triangle, lay out a map of where you fit in that triangle with your partner, extended family, your co-workers, and any other significant relationships. You might play the same role in each arena, or you may switch roles.

Write out how you perpetuate your role in the drama play. Who and what sets you off? What do you do to express that energy or stress? Notice if, in one triangle (relationship), you act in a certain way, but in another, you take on a different role. In other words, do you have a domineering boss (the tyrant), which leads to you being a tyrant at home?

Once you begin to understand the script of your plays, take that awareness into the moments preceding your interactions. Notice what you are feeling, and where in your body you are feeling that emotion. Using your Mindfulness training, allow those sensations some space. Let them release at their own speed.

Once you can stay aware of your need to go into reaction by taking on one of the roles, begin your interaction. Know that you will immediately be thrust back into your role. That is OK. Notice that you have an intention to shift the dance, so that you can step out of that role, even if it is for a moment.

As you go in and out of awareness through your interactions, you will feel the hold of the drama letting go. Speaking from my personal experience, this process can take a while before you feel like things are shifting. It's a learning curve, where the significant change usually doesn't happen immediately.

Others may try to suck you back into the drama. Or they may just relax from you not being charged up with new your role. If you feel the other person(s) are baiting you to keep the drama going, just disengage. You don't need to keep communicating with someone who is trying to suck you back in.

If they relax and you have a relationship where it would be appropriate, tell them what you are doing. You are much more likely to get a favorable response from the other person(s) if they first experience you relaxing and attempting to shift your role.

Starting a conversation from a place of taking responsibility for your part will enable others to do the same. As you explain that so much of the *Drama Triangle* is learned unconsciously as a survival strategy, others are much less likely to feel made wrong. When they know that their behaviors were their best attempts at surviving they won't feel you blaming them, but describing how they did the best they could. You may get to a place where you can all laugh at your tendency to fall into your roles when stressed.

Break out of your box

Before you can break out of your box, you need to know what it is. For at least a week, make notes throughout your day on the rules you follow. You don't need to be obsessive. Notice the ones that produce a feeling—subtle or strong.

For example, observe your driving box. Most of us live in metropolitan areas, where driving is work. Notice what your rules are, particularly under stress. When you're late, the traffic is heavy, and you're tired, what are your rules? "No one can pass me"? "I will only allow one car length between me and the car in front of me"? You get the idea.

As you start detecting your daily boxes, it will be easy to expand to the bigger ones of your life. Those boxes of who you should be as a man. What are your boxes around education, work, marriage, friendship, and family? You will find that some of the boxes represent who you are, and truly serve you.

If you have friends or a partner whom you feel comfortable asking, ask them what they perceive as the rules you live by. Frequently our friends, and certainly our spouse, will have their opinions of us. But don't ask how they feel about you; rather, ask them to tell you what core beliefs they see you operating under.

If you or a friend comes up with a rule that questions your existence, ask a few men. I suggest you speak to other men you respect. If it pertains to your profession, you may want to speak to a few people outside of it. Talk to these men about what your box is. You may tell them how you were bred to be an attorney. Maybe you weren't pushed, but your parents would talk about how great it would be if you were an attorney like your dad.

Peel away your box to see and feel what's been caged. Once you get honest and allow yourself to feel the emotions, you will have an initial urge to act. Take action—not extreme action. I'm not advocating quitting your job to travel off to a remote island. Don't go to work the next day and quit. There is often an opposite emotional reaction to a long period of repression. Let that energy drain out before you change your life.

If, for instance, you went to medical school because it was the right thing to do, and now you realize it's not right for you—express your anger if you need to. Once you release the initial wave of emotions, subtler ones such as grief will come up. As you begin to settle down, go deeper into what you were getting out of your box. What where your secondary gains? What hidden, or not so hidden, benefits were you getting?

Going to medical school got you the approval of your family and our culture at large. What other benefits were you getting? Maybe you didn't have to risk trying to be an artist. As a kid you didn't have much choice, but often as adults we keep behaving as if we don't have a choice. We believe the jail door is locked—when it hasn't been for years.

Deepening who you are
What were your reactions when you read about owning your consequences and where you need to be accountable? Maybe you notice every time you drive into your work parking lot you

feel tense. Or you might feel as you put on your work clothes you're holding your breath as if you are putting on a straightjacket. It could be noticing you spend a lot of time fantasying about starting your own business. Jot those reactions down. Start working those items by following what's laid out in this chapter. Once you create your list, take one item and start working it by seeing how it shows up in your life, and with whom. As you become aware of how it affects you and others, feel your response in your body. What emotions are generated?

If you need to speak to a person to move on, do it. I know it takes balls to do that, and you might screw up when you do it. But just taking action will free you.

When you release the hold a behavior or belief has on you, it may reveal another. For a while it might feel like one risk taken only reveals another. Keep going, it will end—and you come out the other side a free man.

As you create your list of clean-ups, also use the Five Aspects of Self (described earlier in the chapter) to become clear on what you want. You have two lists: the one you are completing and the one you are moving towards. Again, don't be anal. Let the list guide you to carve out the life that you want.

When you encounter a new situation, you will find that the skills you developed from working these lists will automatically kick in. You will know if the situation will take or give you energy. Will it require an inappropriate amount of work, or will it be rewarding? It's not about avoiding work; it's about choosing the right work for you. You start out completing your past, move into directing your future, and evolve to having entirely new skills.

Don't do all this in one week. It is much better to work a few items for a period of time than rush through them all. If you need to take a break, do it. You are doing deep, powerful work. Honor yourself for the courage and perseverance it takes to complete this task. Again, if you can do this with another man, it will be easier and more fun.

I know you can do this. I have seen hundreds of men do it. You and your family, even if it's a future family, deserve this.

Chapter 7:
Go For It! Take Some Risks!

"Only those who will risk going too far can possibly find out how far one can go."

—T.S. Eliot

The Value of Risk

Take an attitude of conscious risk.

Now it starts getting fun.

You've developed skills for being present. You've let go of what's not serving you. You actively sought assistance. You learned how to complete and became more responsible for your own life. Now you start focusing on producing, which is exactly what men do well!

As men we compare, criticize, and compete. You learned by being compared to others, and comparing yourself to others. You also learned by being criticized, prodded, and urged to better yourself. Admit it, we all know that we compete.

These all are instinctual drives. In some men, they're stronger than in others, but it's there for all of us. Clearing out all that crap allows these instincts to work in productive ways. When a man has not done his work and denies those instincts, they become destructive. Those men who haven't matured along their path are the ones who cut other men down because of their jealousy or insecurity.

Own your Shadow, that part of you that hides from your real feelings. Take responsibility for going for what you want. It's less risky to sit on the sidelines and yell insults to the players than to be on the field risking fumbling. But where has yelling from the sidelines ever gotten you?

A man's story

Many years ago Jim came to me distraught. His successful life was no longer successful. He had started and run successful businesses, and he was such a good web designer he could do it in his sleep. In recent years, though, he'd run into some "bad luck." One partner thought "partnership" meant he got the rewards and Jim did all the work. Jim, being a nice guy, went along believing his partner would pay him when they had money. When that day came, and the firm was sold for a good chunk of money, Jim discovered that in the course of developing the company, he had been slowly, legally, edged out. He got nothing.

Jim wrote it off as bad luck, and figured he would make up for it on the next deal, working at another startup. As with most startups, there were all kinds of promises of large rewards. But as things progressed, operating capital began to shrink. Jim's paychecks were delayed, but he eventually got paid. After a few months passed, though, Jim was not getting paid at all. Still, he was a team player, so he kept working, living off of his credit cards and the promise of future payment.

Finally, things came to a head for Jim. The stress of no money, dwindling reserves, increasing debt, and lessening food stores woke Jim up to the common denominator in all these situations: himself. He realized that his whole life was one experience after another of him giving and others taking. The more he felt this, the madder he got. But this time, he took action. He was initially rejected for unemployment, but appealed to the state and won. He compiled evidence and put together a case to sue his former employer. It was such a good case, the business quickly worked out a generous settlement with Jim.

More important than the money, though, Jim got his power back. Because he'd never had it, he didn't know what was missing. Once he got a taste of it, he could not be stopped. The battle for his money was a battle to take back what was his and establish boundaries. After his wins, Jim continued to stand taller and taller. His wife became more admiring and affectionate towards him. He saw himself as a man.

Set boundaries

For many of us, when we learned to be that "sensitive nice guy," we learned to erase our boundaries. We were told—if only indirectly—that having boundaries was a bad thing. We were told they could hurt people, keep others at a distance. We rarely saw men who were powerful, yet gentle in their rightful use of that power.

When I speak to people about setting boundaries, I usually get a negative response, as if setting boundaries harms people. Your boundaries aren't set with anger or the desire to control others, though. Nor are they set solely to keep people out. They're not rigid walls, they're permeable, allowing what serves you to move in and out.

Your boundaries are the edge of your personal power, your personal container. Your acceptance of yourself fills you and your space. They help you own your space. A mature man has a presence about him, and that presence is usually open. It's not defined; you just have to know what is appropriate.

You create these boundaries and this space by doing what you need to do to grow up. You'll create your resource base to cultivate what you need to be a mature man. You'll have sources from which you receive the knowledge and advice you need. You'll cultivate relationships with people who are honest with you, who support you for who you are and what you want to be. You'll invest the time and money to do the work and get the healing you deserve.

When you believe you are worth this investment, you are a mature man. Your actions are saying, "I am valuable and honorable." You use your maturity for your own evolution, and to invest in others. Because you have your own sense of self worth, you are your own man. You don't need others to give you things that you can give yourself. This puts you in a position of power. Without a need for others to give to you, you can choose. Your wants and desires drive you, not your needs.

Purpose

A man without a purpose is lost. He has no guiding star. Being a man is about having purpose. We are about moving our purpose forward.[21]

Purpose is not about changing what doesn't work in your life; it's something bigger than you. It might be simple and clear, like being the best father you can be. It might be as complicated as saving a rare species. Your purpose might make you a little crazy—that's good. If it makes others crazy, that's not so good. But that is one reason they will be attracted to you—because you allow yourself to be out there more than they will let themselves be. So ask yourself, what are you willing to die or live for? What gives you the inspiration to move through those tough times? What are you willing to take risks for?

There are two ways to grow. One is to work on fixing what is broken, or removing the parts that are not what you want. The first part of the book focused on much of that. The other way to grow is to go for your passion, your purpose. The entrepreneur and the artist know this one. When you commit to something bigger than you, your stuff will come up—that personal stuff you need to deal with, outgrow, re-pattern, or release. You will not need to go looking for it. It will be there.

I propose that you travel a third path to growth: do it all together. Fix what's broken, get rid of what isn't working, *and* find and fulfill your purpose. You may need to focus more on

---

[21] In his book *The Way of the Superior Man,* David Deida nails the whole topic. I have seen this book piss men and women off, and I appreciate that he's willing to upset people to wake them up. (Incidentally, many of these people grow to understand and appreciate what he is saying.)

one part to start. That's fine. But at some point you need to get off your ass and start risking. You might say, "I don't know what I want. I'm not excited about anything." OK, that's fair. So go on an exploration. You could travel, but you don't need to. Get involved with new people doing new things. Enroll in classes you wouldn't normally take. Stretch yourself. For instance, if you don't like being touched, take a massage class. If you think you have no musical ability, take a piano class. Nothing is on the line. You're just doing it for yourself. A mature man still has fear—he just doesn't let it stop him from moving forward.

Use the resources at the back of the book to help you discover your purpose, and know that your purpose will evolve and change. When it does change, that's a loss, and with any loss there is grief. If your purpose is done—if your kids are grown and gone, or that endangered species is safe now—allow yourself time to grieve and integrate. A new purpose will appear.

The man who never had a purpose (or, really, just never believed he had one) is in a more difficult situation. Once you have one, you know what it feels like to be alive with a purpose. Even if you aren't yet succeeding with your purpose, you will get energy from it. Women are drawn to men who are going for their purpose.[22] The converse is also true: your wife or partner will complain if you're sitting on your ass.

Whom do you serve?

Until the master you serve is your own purpose, you are not your own man. You may be part of the way there, and that's good. But to fully be a man, you need to be fully in the game—in your game.

---

[22] Deida discusses this in his book, *The Way of the Superior Man.*

You can't be fully in the game if others are in your space uninvited. Set your boundaries, with no excuses and no apologies.

An attitude based on the growing refinement of purpose is powerful and life-affirming. When you allow yourself to set the needed boundaries to pursue your purpose, you fill yourself with what it really means to be a man. When you stop following the masses, stop listening to the limiting messages your mental chatter sends you, and stop worrying about the risks in pursuing your purpose, you will feel that you are a man.

With clarity and his purpose behind him this kind of man has an attitude. He may be viewed as unreasonable by others, based on who he is; he might be a quiet presence or he could be a strong presence. Either way, he is his own man. Either way, his Masculine Emotional Intelligence grows.

Remember that as a young man, let's say up to age thirty, much of your purpose is about adventure, exploring, and having fun. I was abnormal—I stumbled on to my first purpose in my early twenties. For most men it will be later. Go out and create the experiences that will cultivate your purpose.

Purpose leads to passion

Cal Newport's claim to fame was writing and speaking about how to succeed as a student. He would know how—he graduated Phi Beta Kappa from Dartmouth College, then received his PhD from the Massachusetts Institute of Technology. His next endeavor was researching passion. His book, *So Good They Can't Ignore You: Why Skills Trump Passion in the Quest for Work You Love* describes how following your passion is not always the best advice.

Newport discovered that, particularly in the beginning of our career, we aren't able to know what our passion is. It's the struggle of working and building core traits, such as conviction, that evolve to be the foundation for succeeding with our passion later on in our life. Consequently, what you do for a living is much less important than how you do it.

As you grow as a man, you are discovering your purpose. The awakening of your purpose naturally feeds your passion. It's difficult to be passionate about something that doesn't connect to who you are. When you are on your purpose, the passion is there.

A man's story

Jose came to me stressed out from driving a cab in the scorching Arizona summer, and still depressed after three years of weekly therapy. The therapy hadn't given him the clarity he hoped it would. All his hard work as a cabbie and therapy client was only exhausting him.

Gradually, Jose started letting go of what others thought he should be. A decade before I met him, Jose had been an art student in Wyoming. Jose's parents had encouraged him to pursue medicine because they thought Jose would make a good physician. He certainly would have had an exceptional bedside manner, but Jose didn't want to be a doctor, no matter how much his parents would cajole or bribe him. He knew enough to know that his parents' purpose was not his.

Within two months of starting working with me, Jose was enrolled in HVAC (Heating, Ventilating, and Air Conditioning) school. He sailed through the school and quickly opened his own business. He was bright, hard working and good with people, so he was quickly successful.

It only took two years before Jose started working on his next profession, meteorology. Maybe his experience of the Arizona heat inspired his interest in weather. He sailed through his Masters then his Ph.D., and came out of school with a patent for his new instrument to measure temperature change. Applying his HVAC knowledge, he created an entirely new tool.

It took a few years for Jose to unwind himself from his family's and the culture's expectation of him. His stints as a cabbie and HVAC man were not fun, but he didn't give up on himself. In the course of his journey he tried psychotherapy, Rolfing® (SI), numerous courses (such as massage) and more art classes before he settled into his passion and purpose.

We all want to get it easily and quickly. I did. Often the men who get it are the ones who are willing to do the work, whatever it is. For some men, it's changing careers, like Jose. For others it's doing more personal development work. Then for some, sticking it out in one job is exactly what they need to do. As I have said, it is less the "what" than the "how." Jose continued to risk and learn. He could have gone to medical school with his parents footing the bill for school and for setting him up in practice. But Jose chose to do the work, to follow his instincts, and to discover what would give him satisfaction.

Jose is an excellent example of a man who became excellent at what he did—then his passion and purpose found him. Without knowing what his purpose was, Jose let that purpose direct him. That primordial urge to be the man he wanted to be kept him trying the next thing. One of the gifts I was honored to give Jose was the support to keep going for it. I would never have guessed he'd end up as a leading climatology professor. I did see in him that he had a gift to offer the world, but I see that in every man. The difference with Jose was that he was willing to consider that he had something in him that was more than what his parents saw or his jobs required. He was willing to be unreasonable to find his purpose.

Refinements

Once you've defined your purpose, you'll be in a constant state of refining it. Allow yourself to make course corrections. Don't see them as failures; see them as mistakes that are teaching you. What you think you are learning from your "mistakes" often turns out to be wrong, and your bigger lesson was something entirely different that you didn't realize until much later.

Look for distinctions within your purpose, as well as within your entire life. The more seriously you involve yourself in an activity, the finer your distinctions will become. As a skier I learn to make subtler and subtler moves to get the results I want. Continue to notice in yourself how your experience changes as you go through the day. As you develop more precise awareness about your own responses and others', the more effective you will be.

It could be said that growing up is one continuous process of finer and finer distinctions. A mature man uses his developed distinctions to guide him in ways no one else could. You are less reliant on others, particularly our institutions, to direct your decisions. From years of staking out finer and finer qualities, you become your own advisor. You will notice others will seek you out for what you notice.

Remarkable tasks
Exercises to learn, reinforce, and embody your growth as a Remarkable Man

Your purpose
What's your purpose? You don't know? Go find it. If you do know, let's draw it out.

Find a mentor

Your mentor(s) could be anyone, including a woman. I have had some powerful women teachers. I would suggest you have at least 50% of your mentors be men, though.

First, a mentor is a model. In who he is and how he lives his life, he models qualities and behaviors for you. We learn more from watching, copying, and projecting with our models than we learn from didactic instruction. The subtle things we pick up on by hanging out with these men can be the most profound. Many of our fathers didn't really hang out with us as kids. Many men have a latent hunger for what their fathers were unavailable to give. I certainly did.

Relax in the presence of this man. Feel how he is a man. I am not saying be him, but get a visceral sense of how he is a man. When you are with him, how do you feel? Does your heart open? Are you inspired to take action? Do you see things you never saw? Are you more creative? Are you smarter? Are you [fill in the blank of what you want to be]?

Whatever you are feeling is already in you. This man's presence is waking it up in you. It's like a dormant seed being germinated. Your goal is to get to the point where you can sustain that state without your mentor, where you are passionate and creative on your own. Take that seed and plant it where you want it to grow. Go back to your mentor for advice, inspiration, and support as needed.

Maybe it will only take one mentor to awaken your purpose. Or it may take a few to triangulate your purpose. Keep looking for your mentors. Be open to them showing up in unexpected ways. They could as easily be a boss as they could be a friend. They also could be a collective experience like school or a men's group. It might not be one man. I opened up to learn a tremendous amount from my clients. It might be biographies you read or movies you see. All can imprint your unconscious mind with new images and models. Some mentors will be very accepting; others will be challenging. I first needed the accepting ones before I was able to handle the challenging ones.

Expanding our model of mentors, let's include our "enemies." The men who challenge us also, in some ways, represent some hidden parts of ourselves. It might not be a part you want to own or develop, but owning it can empower you.

Developing in the ways our enemies developed usually does not serve us, of course; as with other mentors, these men are there to teach you, but it might only be to help you clarify what you don't want. I also think it's to challenge you to draw out your voice.

I learned that I was more vulnerable to these negative experiences if I was not connected to my purpose. I was more likely to buy into someone else's purpose. In the long run, these experiences taught me more of who I am than the positive experiences. They certainly demanded more of me.

Find a venue
With the help of your mentors, plant your seed. Find a place to allow what's germinating to grow. Commit. Start doing it. Make art. Build something. Write it all down. Just start producing.

You can't manifest your purpose solely in your head. It will come to fruition only because you are out there interacting with others. For many people these days, social media meets that need. There have never been as many ways to connect as there are now.

There is nothing more dear to you, nothing more uniquely who you are, than your purpose, so exposing it can be scary. Like an artist or a musician offering his work to the public, you are setting yourself up to be judged.

You can see how this thrusts you into growing, into growing up, into contributing and into walking your talk. Find a place to display your work!

Expose yourself

Share your art. Once you have your venue, keep displaying your latest work. Become a prolific painter.

Invite people to view and judge your work. Keep breathing! See the entire process as simultaneously a process of growth, creation, and contribution. Your risk-taking will inspire others to take their needed risks. Being unreasonable as you discover your way to being remarkable will be a model for others to do the same

Even with failure, you're offering a gift. The courage it took to offer is always a gift. As men, we are trained to comment on the results, and we don't often honor the courage. So honor your courage.

Doing it

Take your evolving purpose, find a place to plant the seed for it, and then invite others to experience it. If you aren't doing this, create a plan with a timeline to do it. Then find others who you are accountable to. With their support and accountability, start with your first act today, an act beyond just mapping it out. Take action. Make that first call, post that first blog post. Keep taking action every day for ninety days. Even if it's a little thing, just keep working toward your purpose. Remember—it's as much about the journey as it is the goal!

Chapter 8:
Connect to the Divine,
Know You're Not Alone

"A dream you dream alone is only a dream. A dream you dream together is reality."

—*John Lennon*

Connect to the Divine—in yourself and in your relationships with friends and family

While moving through the previous seven steps, you have connected with a deeper part of yourself—and you've connected with others in new, more intimate ways.

Now connect to something beyond this world. Call it whatever you want—God, the Universe, the Creator, Nature, Higher Power, the Divine—any of the various names for what is more than you. It doesn't matter how you label it, but acknowledge it, feel it, and connect to it.

A man's story

For a boy who loved hanging out at the creek enjoying the peace nature offered, parochial school was tough for Ted. He constantly fought with the nuns; everyone was relieved when he decided to attend the local public high school. But college was an awakening for Ted. First, he began to appreciate the good education he got in his Catholic schools. Then, he started to find ways to understand religious teachings that hadn't made sense as a boy. Through asking questions and listening to people of other religious upbringings, Ted decided it was less about the form and more about the connection.

At first, he was amazed that people from India, Africa, and East Asia had such different practices, yet all were connecting to their Creator. Once he saw how others practiced their religions, Ted appreciated his Catholic childhood in ways he never had before. He understood the power of ritual. Those Latin Masses had a new meaning. Ted felt sad that he hadn't had this awareness and appreciation as a boy.

By the end of college, Ted's religious view had come full circle. He didn't call himself a Catholic any longer, but he was a Christian. His agnostic view towards religion evolved into a view based not on intellectual teachings, but on personal experience.

Ted's life took off immediately after graduation. He kept his commitment to himself to travel after college, which led him to work for a high-tech company designing information systems for large international corporations. The job was challenging, profitable, and intense. At the beginning of the week, Ted would be on one side of the planet, and by the end of the week, he was on the other side. Through Ted's passion and brilliance, he was writing his own ticket.

Then he had an opportunity to fulfill a dream he'd always had to start his own company. In spite of the fear of not having all the support of a large corporation behind him, he went for it. In the first three years, he worked harder than he had ever worked.

One day he woke up, and realized he'd made it. His company was successful. His employees were running it without him, and Ted didn't need to work anymore. His whole life he'd wanted to create a successful business that ran itself. Now he had.

At first that was a huge win. But a few days later, he woke up depressed. He and his friends couldn't understand why. He had everything—a great wife and family, a successful business, world travel, and a beautiful home. So why was he depressed?

The more he thought about it, the more depressed he got. He applied his old skill set of brilliance and determination to solving this problem like he'd solved every other problem before in his life. He did his research. He even tried therapy. If Ted was anything, he was open to new experiences. Still he was getting more depressed. He'd go to work, but they didn't need him. In fact, he felt like he was in the way.

Through a Facebook connection to an old college friend, Ted received an offer to visit India. His wife told him to go, in part to get him out of her hair. Ted packed his bags immediately. He was off on an adventure. It felt like the old days of traveling for the hell of it. As the plane left the tarmac some of his depression lifted.

Landing in Mumbai, the cultural shock was a slap in the face. Ted immediately had to deal with the intense chaos. He wasn't thinking of himself any longer. Ted's friend, Gopal, took him into his house and life. They talked shop, reminisced about their days at school, and played tourist. After a few days, Gopal suggested Ted take a little pilgrimage to a Hindu ashram out of the city. Ted was having a good time and had no commitments, so he said sure.

Being at the ashram reminded Ted of his parochial school days. There were strict rules, people walking around in long religious outfits, places of silence, and a lot of religious artifacts. He felt at home. Ted called his wife with more energy in his voice than he'd felt in a long time, asking what she thought of him staying longer. She encouraged him to stay, so he did.

As Ted learned to sit in silence, he felt the depression return. He felt a deep exhaustion consume him. All he was doing was sleeping and sitting. There was nothing else to do. No one needed anything of him. Waves of exhaustion would be followed by waves of sadness. Ted had emotional flashbacks to times in his life when he was too busy to feel his sadness, his fear, and even his anger. But he was feeling it now in the ashram.

Slowly, in between the exhaustion and the emotions, moments of deep peace would magically appear, for no reason Ted could see. He would be walking through the courtyard and notice a flower that had been there for days. Transfixed on the flower and its subtle perfume Ted would recognize that he was happy. In these growing moments of happiness, something else started to appear. He felt a presence he'd never felt. There were moments when his brain would try to figure out what was happening, but Ted would practice the surrendering he was learning, let go of analyzing, and just be.

The passion that Ted had as a young man was back in a new form. It was less about creating and more about being. His drive had returned too, but it was tempered with a peace that he had never had before. On his flight back home, Ted reviewed how he had changed since his flight to India. He started laughing out loud about how he was "just going to visit a friend." He was coming home with an old friend he had lost: a connection to himself and to something beyond himself that he knew on a theoretical level, something that he remembered having as a kid at the creek. He came home *experiencing* what he was just taught in his early schooling.

You probably have had some kind of spiritual or religious aspect to your life before now. Whether that was a pleasant or an unpleasant experience, you can let it go, because now you get to reinvent your spiritual experience. There are no rules here; there's no "right" way to do this. If you're feeling a little lost, though, check out my website, OwenMarcus.com, for some suggestions. Some men develop a deeper relationship with nature. Others find a mission to give back to their community. Some men feel the connection through ceremonies, prayer, or meditation. For others it can be subtler, producing no outward changes, just a new inward sense.

However you do it, deepening your divine connection is not something you do alone. In the arrogance of youth, a lot of us believed it was just us, that there was nothing bigger than who we were, no Creator or Divine guidance. We were the only ones who knew what was going on. When you connect to the Sacred, you have more peace, feel a deeper sense of purpose, and have more clarity in your life. You know you're not alone. We're *all* connected. You don't need to *believe* in a higher power to feel more powerful when you have a connection beyond yourself. You aren't doing it alone.

As for Ted, he went back to work—but not as a manager at his company. He continued to let his company run itself, and he started a new social entrepreneurial endeavor. He became a leader of change. He applied his knowledge of business and information systems to create a better way to monitor water quality for streams. Connected to the Divine, he connected to Nature and his World Community. And he felt fulfilled. He gave back to that creek that gave him so much as a boy.

Accountability to your standard

As men we want power. As we mature as men, we want the power to be righteous. To be honorable in your use of power, it helps to be accountable. An immature man evaluates everything from a perspective of what it will do for him. As this man matures, he sees that his actions have consequences beyond him. He often looks for support in determining what is right and in achieving it. I know I am more likely to do the right thing if I know my action will not only have a consequence, but that I am being held accountable to a standard beyond myself—a standard I set with and shared with others.

It is often in that middle stage of Evolutionary Change, the Catalyst Stage, when you make your connection to your Creator. During that dark night of the soul, you surrender like you have never surrendered before. By relinquishing what was not you, what was not working and what were others' values, you come out not only stronger but connected. Ted slowed down enough for his life to catch up to him so he could truly live it.

Ted will undoubtedly have failure in his life, as will you. But when you fail with a connection to your Sacred, it's not as lonely or hopeless. In those moments when you feel all alone, there will be a presence. You will know that someone has your back.

Now you realize that you needed to experience that arrogance of youth, and all the other things you went through in your life, to have the wisdom of maturity. Wisdom comes from experience; it's different from intelligence acquired from knowledge. It's also different from beliefs based on experiences as a victim. Wisdom grounded in life experience is complete, a solid base to stand on. Now you get to partner up with something more. In this step, you're being called for something bigger. Before, you were serving yourself. Now you get to take that wisdom to serve others.

Often at this step, men become the leaders of their community. When you reach this step, others start seeking your council because of the journey you traveled. You earned their respect by staying true to yourself. You did your work. You didn't sell out. You came back from your falls stronger. You matured.

Contribution

When I listen to men of all ages, I hear that they want to make a contribution. Young men have a burning passion to contribute, to make a difference. Middle-aged men want to achieve the goals that will be their contribution and older men want to guide others in achieving their contributions.

Younger men don't know *if* they can, or *how* they can, contribute. Middle-aged men lose their focus on the prize of contributing in their quest to provide for their families and themselves. Older men deal with the grief of where they dropped the ball, and where they tried but fell short.

You see where I am going. Within this triad of life stages are opportunities. When the older men allow themselves to reconnect to their passion and innocence through connecting with younger men, magic happens. Younger men don't need to be told *how* to do it. They may ask specific questions, but they don't need to be directed. They need to try, fail, and succeed in their own way. These older men get to heal their grief from not always being the man they hoped to be through their contributions. Part of their gift to younger men is their acceptance of their failures. Young men struggle, worrying about failure. They struggle with how to get up after failure. If only by the virtue of age, an older man knows how to get back up, and can teach that to young men.

What better person to reach out a hand to a young man than a man who fell many times himself? In offering to help—which might mean just being there for a young man—it shows the young man that there is no shame in failing. Failure is a needed part of life. It teaches us, it heals us, and it loves us with its humbling lessons.

For the older man, hanging out with a young man brings him back to that part of his life. It rekindles his passion and innocence. He remembers what it was like to have a dream to make a difference. He recalls what it meant to commit his whole life to something bigger than himself. He remembers the fear and excitement of not knowing how he was going to make it happen. All this transforms his grief into hope. Being the guide gives the older man new purpose.

I saw this with my father. At the end of his career as a business executive, he took great pride and enjoyment in mentoring his younger employees. He had patience and commitment to further their success. He got to return the support he received when he was younger. My dad would go on about one of his employees as a proud parent goes on about his child. It wasn't patronizing—it was respecting the unique gifts each one possessed.

Now that I am an old man (by this standard), I notice how I have an instinctual need to contribute to young men. I occasionally have to remind myself to shut up and listen. They remind me to *be*—not to *do*. My best advice comes when I am asked for it, not when I offer it. Starting my men's groups and training other men to lead groups is part of my giving back, as is writing this book. Even more than the specific advice in this book, which there is a lot of, I want to have all men sense the power of giving and receiving presence. Being with another man and accepting him is more powerful than any advice.

The middle-aged man is situated between having an all-encompassing dream (or a desire for that dream) and grieving for not fully achieving that dream. He either is or isn't succeeding at achieving his dream of contributing. He may have given up on that dream for another dream of a family, professional success, money, or the pursuit of pleasure.

In some ways, the dream is an excuse to get off our ass to experience life. Then we meet life, and it can be hard and mean. Life demands from us things we may not know we have to give. It wants us to provide and protect our family, to succeed, to grow, and—if there is time and energy left—to live our dream. We can't do it all. No man can. But we need to *believe* we can— that innocence of youth needs to be naive. We need to have a dream of life that is bigger than our experiences in the container of life.

Not only do we make mistakes, we make compromises. For some of us, it's a daily trickle of passion leaking out of our dream bucket. For others it is the allure of the material world. Then for some, it is having life demand what you never expected. Maybe you have a special needs child, maybe you become seriously ill, maybe your successful business suddenly, inexplicably fails. How you deal with those challenges shapes you and helps define who you become as a man.

A man in the middle is a "dog soldier," the Cheyenne Indian term for the man who fights until the end. He just keeps working, often not knowing why. For many men, there is no awareness of what occurred until he reaches the next step. He hopes his actions will produce what he needs and wants. If not, he might work harder.

This whole step is critical to a man's maturity; it is when he comes to discover that there is more than the material world. Life whittles away the parts that are not truly you, and it carves out a real man. As those old parts fall away, you may miss them. You believed that those parts defined you as a man. They did for a while, and you may fight against a redefinition of who you are. At some point, you will surrender to the death of the man you thought you wanted to be, and become the man you are meant to be.

This middle journey will allow you to be the older man with the grace of acceptance that you can offer to younger men. Here is a secret for young men: the more you allow older men to assist you, the more successful you will be, and the struggle of your middle years will be less. When the innocence of youth transforms into the arrogance of middle age, it makes life tough. I know, because I believed I knew it all. I believed I didn't need help. I worked harder than I needed to work. So fully live every step. Don't rush it. Ask for, receive, and give help.

In aboriginal societies, the elders of the tribe are honored by all. The young warriors may do some rebelling, but they come back to the elders for guidance. The elders know, from being there themselves, that a young man, and even a middle-aged man, needs to fail to succeed; it is his choice if he does it with grace and ease. It is his choice if he allows for something greater than himself to assist him, if he allows other men to help him, if he allows for the possibility and the experience of a phenomenon bigger than himself.

Your divine connection

By connecting to the Creator, you might find that piece that was always missing. It might feel like it finds you. Sometimes it feels like you found a partner to co-create with. It might be that you found someone or something to serve. Giving your unique gifts warms your heart in ways nothing else can.

Seeing how your life experience and your purpose are needed in the world can feed a hunger inside you that might have existed for decades, a hunger you didn't even know about. Whether you feel the connection through a direct experience with your Creator or from a worldly experience—like teaching children to read—just find a way to feel it. Seek out and experience a deeper connection to God, and you will move to a whole new level of being a man.

With your connection to your divine, your contributions become richer for both you and those you serve. You are less likely to be burnt out when you are living your purpose, connected to your Creator and giving your unique gifts. In fact, I can't think of a more powerful way to renew your soul than doing those three things.

Remarkable tasks

Exercises to learn, reinforce, and embody your growth as a Remarkable Man

Answer these questions to awaken that connection in you. If it is awake, good—now nourish it into being an integral part of you as a man. Find places that allow you to express this connection, while supporting you to deepen it. Don't be limited by your traditional religion. What works for one man may not work for you.

Find your divine:

1. What moves you?

2. What scares you about what is more than you?

3. When you have no one else to talk to, what do you do? When you are desperate, who do you talk to?

4. By the Steps:
   a. If you are a young man: what are your dreams? How do you want to contribute? What older men can you ask to mentor you?

   b. If you are in the middle: what is your struggle? What dreams, hopes, or ways of contributing have you had to put aside? What are your feelings about doing this? What would it take to forgive yourself, let go, and start from here?

   c. If you are an older man: where have you fallen short relative to your expectations? To whom can you contribute?

Once you have deepened your connection to your Creator, do something with it. As men we *do*. In the doing we put into action our purpose and feel our connection with what is beyond us.

There are two scary parts of ourselves to share. One is our love for our purpose, and the other is our love for our connection to the divine. Because both of these parts are deep and private in how they represent the essences of who we are, sharing them with others can be challenging.

Through risking and sharing you expand the essence of who you are. You can hide the most precious parts or you can open up to share them. I know I needed to take that leap when I started the most recent men's groups. I needed to practice what I have taught. Over the course of a month, I designed the group I wanted to be in. I wanted a group of deeply committed men who respected each other and didn't waste time telling stories. I wanted men who would challenge me in a loving way. Most of all, I wanted a group where I had to show up 100%. I wanted a group where I needed to share my purpose and my connection to the sacred.

I knew if I was to have that group of men, I needed to be that man first—I needed to model it. In the face of no other man doing it, I had to do it. It was a stretch, but it was exhilarating, too. I figured that, in the worst case scenario, the men I invited would politely refuse. But they went for it. They were as hungry as I was for more out of life.

Over the years we have mentored each other to be our own Remarkable Men. We have taught each other what we never had taught to us. Men have found, changed, and evolved their purposes. Men have discovered their own connections to Spirit, and we have all shared those discoveries with each other.

If you're looking to discover your purpose and your divine connection, find or create the environment you need to help these things grow. It takes a community to grow a Remarkable Man. Find or create your tribe so you can receive that support and give your support to other men.

Contribute your gift

What do you want? What do you need to contribute? With your purpose, your mission in life, what is your contribution? It will change as you change. Right now what do you wake up and go to bed thinking about? What do you find yourself doing naturally? Are you the first person to help a child? Are you the man others go to when they have a relationship problem? Are you the guy who is the business resource for your friends? What are you doing now? What are you jealous of others having or doing—the guys who always get recognized for saving the environment, or maybe the men who all the kids run to be with?

Use your response to these questions to guide you into deepening your connection to your current natural contribution. If you need to do primary work (such as, in my case, starting a men's group), do it. Take that Remarkable Man you want to be with your contributions and put them into action. Let your actions be the canvas on which you paint your passion, purpose, and contribution. Show it off to others. Allow people to be attracted to it.

Every man has gifts to share. This sharing invokes your Remarkableness. Go for it.

Chapter 9:
Enjoy!

"Just play. Have fun. Enjoy the game."

—Michael Jordan

Receive your rewards

Receiving sounds easy, but let's get honest, guys: we're great givers, but receiving compliments, love, or help can be hard. We all need to work on this.

Why is it so hard to receive? Because to receive is to surrender. You don't like the sound of that, do you? Merriam-Webster defines surrender as giving up "completely or agree to forgo especially in favor of another" (maybe your purpose?) and, giving up the fight or control. It's true—to fully receive you have to give up control. You relax and let the other person(s) do his or her thing, whether it's a simple compliment from your friend or your partner showing her love for you in public.

Your ability to receive is directly related to your ability to relax; a tense body is in the autonomic state of fight-or-flight. When you're tense, you're on alert, ready to fight or run, and you're not capable of being vulnerable. Unconsciously, others pick this up. When you're tense, you're sending a signal to others to stay away, because they can sense that you're ready to fight or run. You're on alert even if you don't think you are.

Let's be clear: there is nothing wrong with being strong and having people respect you. But there are downsides to strength *based on tension*—strength based on your ability to fight or escape. With this kind of strength, people stay away. There is an invisible wall between you and others. If you are one of these men, I bet you don't even know it. You're so used to that wall, you don't know what's missing.

A man's story

Andy was the CEO of a Fortune 500 company when he came to me for Rolfing® (SI). He had started at the bottom and worked his way to the top. Gregarious and funny, he's someone both men and women like and respect. When he came to me, he had one problem: his life felt hollow. In spite of his success and popularity, he was bored and lonely.

Andy began to realize that he was always "on." He was always performing, working, watching. His style worked well for him, but he was never relaxed. As he relaxed, he slowed down... and immediately experienced a hum of anxiety. Then he realized something: he was *tired*. It took a lot of energy to always be "on." He also realized that he was sad because of his isolation. To his credit, he allowed himself to surrender to his anxiety, tiredness, and sadness. For the first time he experienced all those emotions. He believed me when I told him it would pass, and it did.

As Andy's energy came back, he was relaxed. He found himself listening more actively. When his secretary spoke to him, he actually heard her now. The same thing was happening with his wife, who told him that she felt closer to him. Andy said, "I didn't do anything. I was just listening." But he was finally *receiving* what his wife had to say. The tension in their marriage dissolved away with Andy's dissolving tension.

Men are hard-wired to be providers and protectors. We do it as an offering of love to those we care about, to those in our realm of responsibility. But it can be hard to shift our focus, hard to take off our battle gear (give up the fight), so we get stuck in the mindset that threat is imminent.

You need to relax more than you realize. When I started this journey thirty-five years ago, my first shock was how tense I was—and I was only in my early twenties! I consistently hear from my clients how surprised they are at the extent of their tension and the tension's impact throughout their bodies—and their lives. And that brings us full circle, back to Step 1: being present. When you are relaxed and present, others want to be with you, others want to give to you.

On one of his earliest trips to the US, His Holiness the Dali Lama spoke in the gym at the University of Colorado on a hot summer day in 1980. I was living in Boulder at the time, so I was lucky enough to hear him speak. He packed the place. In that sweltering gym, he spoke and gave of himself for a couple of hours. He then offered to bless anyone who wanted to be blessed, and I think everyone got in line for that. That day more than thirty years ago changed my life as I witnessed a man who was totally committed.

In 1998, I had the chance to meet His Holiness again at a private reception in a house in L.A. This encounter was very different than the first time around. But even with a hundred cops, Secret Service officers, and SWAT team helicopters circling overhead, this meeting with His Holiness was an even deeper experience for me of this powerful man.

He came into the living room—where less than twenty guests waited—and immediately greeted everyone. In that moment, I felt what true relaxed power really is. This is a man who led an escape from China as a child, continues to rule his people in exile, and is the world's embodiment of peace. He had nothing to prove. He was just being with us, and apparently enjoying himself, because he laughed several times a minute. Yet he commanded the respect of everyone in the room.

It would be wonderful to reach that level of peaceful power in this lifetime. I don't know if I will. But that day, by watching and feeling his model, I made a decision to go in that direction of being a Remarkable Man.

A mature man has the power he needs, so he can relax. So how do you relax when you feel like you *don't* have any power? You relax into what you are experiencing *right now*. His Holiness readily admits his imperfections, and says he got to be who he is through his practice of mindfulness, through his practice of accepting whatever was true for him in the moment. You can become peacefully powerful by allowing whatever is occurring to simply occur. Surrender to your experience. Being with yourself invites others to be with you, as well as themselves.

Once you develop your receiving muscles, you are in a powerful place to give. It is a mature man who has gifts to give. These are the men from whom others seek council: the elders, wise men, or shamans of the tribe. His Holiness has to receive a lot: he needed help along the way in escaping China, now in ruling from exile and in serving others.

You don't have to be a Buddhist leader to experience the joys of the power of receiving and giving. One of my clients, Andy, discovered that listening to people was fun. He didn't have to do anything. He didn't have to be "on." He just received their presence—and his charm was even stronger. Looking people in their eyes, receiving whatever they had to offer, made him more accessible and more powerful. People trusted him even more. He became one of those wise men, an elder of the tribe.

Let go to receive

I still occasionally default to resistance when someone wants to give to me. So before I open my mouth to reject what's being offered, I remind myself that I am safe, I can surrender, and I can breathe and receive. I am getting better at it, and though I am not yet proficient, I am moving in the direction I want to go.

In order to give, you need to be present, let go of what didn't work, and be open to what might occur. You can't possess this level of powerful presence unless you have in some way walked the paths of the first eight steps. The more you really live those other Steps, the more you are able to be vulnerable to receiving. Rather than worrying about giving unconditionally all the time, learn to *receive* unconditionally.

One way to view receiving is that it is the ultimate expression of generosity. How do you feel when someone accepts whole heartedly what you are offering them? Receiving *is* giving a great gift to another.

A man who increases his ability to receive increases his Masculine Emotional Intelligence. The more you receive, the more you can contribute. Just as it takes a community to grow a Remarkable Man, it takes receiving for that man to make his difference in the world. Transforming your ability to receive compliments, direction, support, and just plain help will leverage what you are doing into having a bigger impact.

Remarkable tasks
Exercises to learn, reinforce, and embody your growth as a Remarkable Man

Listening
Once a day, slow down and listen—even if it's listening to someone on the phone. Don't multi-task. When you have thoughts and feelings that take you out of the moment, just let them move through you. Don't focus on them, try not to judge yourself for having them, just let them be.

After your listening experience, ask yourself what did I receive? What did the person give me intentionally and unintentionally? She may have simply explained how to perform a task with a new program, but she also may have expressed her need to be of service by giving her help. Feel those emotional gifts. Take a little more in with each breath.

You know how it feels to help someone with a process you're excited about; you want to pass on that excitement. Receive what others want to give to you, even if *they* are unaware of it. It is a rare honor to be received by a person who is present.

Do this for a week. You can do more than once a day, if you wish. Remember that it is not about quantity, it is about quality. One small interaction where you are fully present is much more powerful than ten conversations that are only slightly more intimate than before.

Give compliments

Give a stranger a compliment as if you are placing an offering at an altar in a shrine. Do this once a day for a week. If a complete stranger isn't around, pick someone you wouldn't normally converse with. Give the compliment, then step back and receive the pleasure you caused. Allow yourself to feel the pleasure—and possibly the discomfort—from this intimate act.

Conclusion

Putting it all together to become remarkable

So, are you a man now? If you're like me, you're a work in progress. As you have read, growing up means learning what you didn't get to learn, then practicing it. It's a process.

Use the Nine Steps to guide your journey. Now that you've read the book, develop your own plan of action. Use the exercises described in Remarkable Tasks to hone your skills. Use the resource chapter. Go to OwenMarcus.com for ideas, refreshers, help, and to connect with others. Participating with others while you grow will exponentially increase your success rate and make it more fun. Remember that you are learning, and learning takes practice. Practice may be boring or tough, but it's the only way to "get good" at anything. Try thinking of it as "I get to" rather than "I have to."

There are times when you will be cruising along with no effort. Then, there will be those times when you feel stalled. Pull out this book to help you refocus and guide you through the tough times. Know that you are reformatting your life. There will be glitches. Some of the old programs will not run on this new operating system.

If you take on the Nine Steps in a serious way, particularly as a means to enrich your life, you are changing from the inside out. You are not simply learning a better coping mechanism; you are disassembling your old world to create a new one that is you. In your new world, you are your own man, and your orientation and actions come from your inner integrity.

For you younger men, keep in mind that many of the later steps will not be directly applicable to you yet. Knowing about them will prepare you. When new stages greet you, rather than react with surprise and avoidance, you could react with excitement and surrender. When I was a younger man, if someone had given me this guide with the Nine Steps, I still would have made mistakes, but I would have learned more easily and quickly! Plus, I wouldn't have felt so alone on the journey.

Reinforce it

Own it

Be that man you want to be. Allow yourself to change. Use this book, others' support, and men you respect to model what you want to be. Then take on what feels right for you.

Even with this book as your guide, you'll need to find men who will model who you want to be and/or be your mentor. I learned to ski by skiing behind guys who were better skiers than I was. Skiing lessons made my dyslexic brain and body just more frustrated. Letting my conscious mind take the back seat and my kinesthetic sense guide me taught my body what to do.

Choose a chapter or an aspect of the book and focus on what you want to achieve with it. Then go out and find real-world models for it. Practice what you're learning first, if you can, in non-critical areas. After skiing behind better skiers, I went out and practiced without following anyone on easier slopes. I could slow it down, concentrate on the subtleness of what I was learning, in the absence of pressure. I could mess up and not injure my body or my ego.

You learn better in a relaxed situation—when you get to the point where performance is *less* important than just being. When you're *not* focused on the external—such as how you look, or the outcome—you are more likely to really integrate your lesson. When you stay in the moment, you are learning on an unconscious level.

When I taught super-Type-A professionals how to transform their stress, I repeatedly told them *not* to practice when they were under severe stress. You have to be relaxed to master it. Students reported back that their "relaxed competence" was unintentionally manifesting changes while under stress. Stress wasn't taking them over like it used to.

Men want to power our way through things, right? Well, you *can* power your way through the steps in this book, and you *will* see results. But if you want to see deep, sustainable results, then allow yourself to be fluid. Have fun with your learning. Make it your own. See all the components as opportunities to new experiences. Make it a sport.

Share it
Part of what got us in trouble in the past was that we were all trying to be someone else's model of a perfect man. But that old model is dying out. It will be replaced, and your most precious contribution can be the subtlest: to be yourself.

As you discover your own unique form of masculinity, you will be transforming the planet. Men want to *do*, to contribute, fix something, change something—and that is all necessary, but it can also reinforce the old model and its problems. When your focus is on doing, you can end up doing something that you later discover was not in yours or others' best interest. Just *being* is incredibly powerful.

As Gandhi said: *"Be the change you want to see in the world."* By embodying your Remarkableness you are walking the talk, and I guarantee that you will be making a difference. By modeling your own unique unreasonableness, you show other men that it is OK to be themselves, to stretch their limits. As an old friend once told me, "If you aren't pissing someone off, something's wrong." You don't *need* to upset others to create change in you or outside of you, but don't hold back your remarkableness out of trying to avoid upsetting someone.

Remember the doctor who, at the pinnacle of his career, realized he'd climbed the wrong mountain? When you are *doing* while you are staying present (*being*) to your evolving purpose, you will be climbing the right mountain. The climb will be easier, quicker, and more productive. It will certainly be more enjoyable for you, and you'll be more fun to be with. Men will want to learn from you because they will want what you have: passion and purpose. Discovering your own dream as you go can be scary, but it's also exciting. Waking up with a little fear of the unknown is much more fun than waking up to another day of despair.

Want to raise the bar? Teach what you are learning. Being and doing it is much better than just studying it. To master it, teach it to others. Learn it as if you had to teach it. Then teach one skill. You could teach it to your son. You could teach it to your interested friend or co-worker. Contribute to someone else's life and your own at the same time through teaching. You can do it. Stretch yourself to be that Remarkable Man.

Join a men's group. If there's no group nearby, check out Men Corps at www.mencorps.org. Make growing up a team sport.

Be an elder

In one of the shamanic lineages I studied, at age fifty-six you were considered an elder. Personally, I see it less as a defined age and more as a state of being. An elder is a man who is mature, who is not focused on proving anything. He's a man who has gained wisdom from his life experiences. He continues discovering life through the ongoing process of mastering his Remarkableness.

An elder will often listen more than he speaks. He might just be the impartial witness to someone, or be giving acknowledgement to another. He guides more than directs. He encourages others to go out and live, to have those experiences that shape a man's life. An elder may even encourage men to take stupid risks when they are particularly young. His stories are allegories for the younger man. More than anything, he models being a man with the dings and dents a man acquires from living.

When you're with a true elder, you know what this man says is true for him. He will honor his word. If he says he will have your back, he will have your back.

Deepen it

To reinforce your maturity and deepen your understanding and practice of each step, go back once you have learned a step to see what more you can learn or apply. Find other support or experiences to enhance what you are learning. If you are like other men I know (including myself), being accountable to someone helps. Having an accountability buddy who is working the steps in the book can be a great asset. Again, there is nothing better than a regularly scheduled men's group to hold you accountable, teach you, support you, model for you, and give you a safe place to practice.

Give the book to your partner so that she understands what you are doing. It will also give the two of you a shared foundation, along with a common language, to communicate with each other. Use the book as way to deepen understanding, communication, and intimacy.

NOTE: I warn both of you not to use the book as a set of standards or an instruction manual. And do *not* make your partner your accountability buddy. The people holding you accountable need to be impartial third-parties.

Remarkable tasks
Exercises to learn, reinforce, and embody your growth as a Remarkable Man

Live your vision of Remarkableness
Use the vision you created at the end of Chapter 6, or go back now and create a vision of who you are as a man. Integrate what you are learning to expand it to be a vision of the man you truly want to be. Leave out those aspects that others want you to be that are not you.

Describe a perfect day for this man. Paint a picture, write a description, or make a vision board (a collage of photos or clippings illustrating your vision) of who this man is. What is he doing and with whom? Concentrate deliberately and visualize yourself as this man. The more you put into developing this vision, the more quickly it will become real.

Go on an exploration discovering who this man is. Find men who possess attributes you want to have. Interact with life from this new vision. Notice how the old version of you wants to jump in, but instead, step back to create space for the new vision to show up. Nurture this new vision as you would nurture your son learning how to swing a bat. Have patience.

No matter what your age, you can reinvent yourself. Having an evolving vision will quicken the process. Don't take yourself too seriously. Laugh at your stupid mistakes. See it as a game where no matter what happens you are winning.

Seth Godin puts it this way: "Don't choose your dreams based on what is certain to happen, choose them based on what's likely to cause the change you want to occur around you."

There are three key components to creating your vision:

1. **Vision**: Clarify what you want.

2. **Clearing:** Remove (let go of) what is preventing you from having it.

3. **Manifest**: Do the work to make it happen.

Clarity of vision
Use what you created from the *Remarkable Tasks* at the end of Chapter 6. Get passionate and take some risks. Let your vision, mission, and purpose live. Invest in them as if your life depended upon it. Take a stand for them.

I am the first to say that even though passion can be key for some people, it's not enough by itself. Excavating your purpose will give you more. Use feedback from others you respect—and from your own experiences—to tweak your vision. The feedback might be "negative;" doing something right now wouldn't be wise. If so, great! You found out before you did it. I believe that behind a bad idea is a better one! I've had many ideas that I thought were genius... only to be proven wrong. I don't necessarily have fewer bad ideas now, I'm just better at listening to the subtle feedback sooner.

This is a vital point about visions: be willing to walk away if it ultimately doesn't serve you. If getting that vision means compromising your principles or purpose, is it worth it? Also, *achieving* that vision might not be as important as *how* you get it. Sometimes, what you *really* wanted to have, learn, or become was buried in the journey. Sometimes, mid-stride, you'll realize you already *have* what you were searching for. Accept it, appreciate it, and let go of the outcome.

At one point in my life, I had to let go of a dream: building the Scottsdale Institute for Health and Medicine. Ultimately, what it came down to was me fulfilling my vision at the cost of my principles and happiness. So I let go of that vision.

Risk

Being your own Remarkable Man is not about "fixing" yourself, people around you, or society. It means stepping into who you are as a man. You may need to clear some space to have room to take your stand. You may need to stop to deal with a problem. That's just all part of your journey as you move forward through your Nine Steps, through your Remarkable life. Ultimately, your life, the model you set, will be something that changes other people around you.

Be a man in a new way. Be *unreasonable.* Speak a truth that you haven't spoken. Get honest with yourself or someone else. Honesty doesn't have to be negative; it could be a positive comment to another man, thanking him for the contribution he made to your life.

Take a stand for something that means a lot to you. Or stand up for a better relationship with your partner. Taking risks by expressing your truth is the fast track to growing as a man.

The other fast track is living your vision. As a Remarkable Man, your focus is your *purpose* represented in your vision. Being a man who lives for something beyond his corporeal self to serve his evolving purpose is the model all men need—and the model the planet needs.

Be Remarkable

You deserve to be the man you want to be. It is your birthright. It is also your biggest contribution to humanity. Take a moment and think about—or better yet, write down—why being that man is important to you and others. As you invest in yourself, what will improve? What difference are you making in your life and the lives of others? How will your relationships improve? How will your kids develop to be the adults you want them to be? What possible impact will you have on your community if you were that man? Do you have a man like that in your life? If so, how can you learn from him? And how can you support and honor him? If not, how will you be that man for yourself and others?

Developing your Masculine Emotional Intelligence is your birthright. Unlearn what doesn't serve. Remember: you aren't bad or broken. You just never got to learn what you needed to learn to be a man with high Masculine Emotional Intelligence. Use this book as your guide to being that Remarkable Man.

Thank You

Thank you for taking the time to read this book. My hope is that you begin to apply it to your life. I appreciate your investment in me and what I had to say. Even more, I appreciate your investment in yourself.

It has been an honor to write for you.

Resources for the Remarkable Man

Tools for being Remarkable

What man doesn't like tools? Well here are some of the tools you can use to re-build yourself as a Remarkable Man. In my experience I've found these tools to be very effective, and you may find other similar tools that serve the same purpose for you.

Let's go right to the cheapest and most powerful tool: a men's group—or, as we call them, a "micro," as in micro-community. You read throughout the book how a men's group will give you what you need; well, we created a nonprofit and site where you can download a free guide to start and run your own men's group. Go to www.mencorps.org to download the guide. Other men are starting their own groups. You can too!

In Chapter 6, I laid out the template for getting clarity about who you are. Using that same template, let's organize your tools.

Spirit

Spirit is that part of you that is more than you. With Spirit being such a personal and unique aspect, there is not much to offer as a resource other than what I mentioned in Chapter 8. You need to go out and experience life to develop this aspect of yourself.

Of course, there are traditional religions with their churches, synagogues, and mosques. But more men are exploring experiences that weren't a part of their upbringing, such as a silent meditation retreat, or exploring Native American traditions.

Many men take on a "spiritual path" as an aspect of their development to their Remarkableness. You could incorporate meditation, ceremonies, a teacher, or a devotional service as a catalyst to take you deep within yourself.

There is no single way. It comes down to what draws you in and opens you up. Men who focus on developing their spiritual side do so because the tradition they are using as their guide has deep meaning to them. My suggestion is to ask your friends —both male and female—about their traditions. People generally want to share their experiences, and introduce you to their traditions. Try a few. Go to a new church, do a Sweat Lodge, or take a meditation class. With many of these experiences, you don't need to believe or practice the tradition to attend an event or two. But if you discover that you want more, ask if there is a lineage behind what is being taught that you can explore.

Here are a few examples of non-traditional practices and traditions, and please forgive my brevity:

Buddhism continues to grow in popularity. Just like Christianity there are many sects. Vajrayāna Buddhism or

Tantric Buddhism includes Tibetan Buddhism with their leader, His Holiness the Dali Lama. Zen Buddhism is associated with Japan. Buddhism and, in particular, Vipassana (also called the Insight Meditation), is associated with the practice of mindfulness—being present in the moment.

Hinduism brought us yoga, which for some can become a spiritual devotion.

The native traditions are much less organized than religions. There are many opportunities to experience indigenous practices, but you need to work a little harder to find them.

Emotions

More than just psychology, more than the mental understanding of your emotions, here I'm talking about how you live your emotional life and experience your relationships with others.

Many centuries ago, we in the West separated the body and the mind. Often more associated with women, emotions were viewed as what got in the way of a woman's reasoning. After centuries of having our emotions shut down, and having no models of how to enjoy them, we are lost. When women took their power back, they brought back emotions for all of us. First men tried to find our emotional selves through women— but then we lost our masculine expression of any emotion.

By the late twentieth century, the way to "deal with emotions" was to go into therapy—which can work. But most often, men enter therapy because they're already in crisis. These days, more and more men are either turning to other interventions or getting proactive to heal themselves and learn how to have a healthy emotional life.

With the new masculinity, men are now seeking a non-feminine emotionality, a masculine way of being emotionally expressive. After centuries of repression, we are reinventing it and teaching each other. For years, men were allowed to be happy, funny, or angry—sad, depressed, or needy were simply not permitted in "real men." Now, when I look back over the last thirty-five years, I can see the progress. The fact that we as men want to find our own emotional being is a huge development.

In his book *The Social Animal: The Hidden Sources of Love, Character, and Achievement, New York Times* columnist David Brooks writes about the power and importance of our emotions and unconscious. He freely admits that as a man he is able to write about emotions, but he has yet to develop the depth of expertise with emotions that he has with his mind. But he can—and you can. Just use some of these out-of-the-box approaches.

Here is an overview of opportunities to enhance your emotional being:

Therapy
When you were growing up, your mind and your emotions were probably lumped together as being the same. On top of that, psychotherapy has traditionally disconnected itself from the body. This belief, that the conscious mind is in charge, is the epitome of the old masculine control perspective.

I have seen therapy that works amazingly well for hundreds of clients and students—therapies that integrate other aspects of the self. These therapies tend to be less traditional talk-therapy and more education. The more you expand the scope of the therapy, the more graceful, powerful, and sustainable the therapy. Frequently the "therapy" is not so much a therapy as it is a guided exploration.

Jungian Therapy

Developed by Swiss psychiatrist Carl Jung, a contemporary of Sigmund Freud, Jungian Therapy uses the unconscious, dreams, and archetypes to guide clients to a higher state of wellness. Although it's a classic therapy, it's still considered nontraditional. There are some good Jungian therapists who don't view psychological issues as pathologies.

International Association for Analytical Psychology (IAAP) www.iaap.org.

Ericksonian Hypnosis

Ericksonian Hypnosis was developed by dyslexic psychiatrist Dr. Milton Erickson on the premise that it is our unconscious that is in charge. Erickson was a master at not only understanding the unconscious mind, but at using "indirection hypnosis" to effect deep change quickly. Erickson practiced in Phoenix, and passed away around the time I moved there, so I got to work with a few of his patients and students. Their stories would have you believing he was a sorcerer.

NLP (Neuro Linguist Programming)

NLP is a learning and psychology approach that is not usually seen as therapy, but was developed, in part, from Milton Erickson's ability to speak to the unconscious. When you know how to listen and watch the subtle cues a person expresses, you can build deep rapport to create significant change.

Since I began studying Ericksonian Hypnosis and NLP in the early 1980s, both of these approaches have become semi-mainstream. Every community should have practitioners.

The Milton H. Erickson Foundation
www.erickson-foundation.org
602-956-6196

NLP Comprehensive
www.nlpco.com
800-233-1657

NLP Connection, an online forum
www.nlpconnections.com

Core Transformation
www.coretransformation.org

Body Centered Therapy (somatic psychotherapy)
Body centered therapies are what they sound like—they use the body as an integral part of the therapy. Some integrate bodywork in the therapy, others track the body as part of the therapy. All see the body, mind, and emotions as aspects of the same phenomenon.

***Hakomi Therapy (mindfulness therapy*)**
Wilhelm Reich was an Austrian-American psychiatrist who was the first to bring the body into therapy. An old friend of mine, Ron Kurtz, took the best of Reich's work, integrated mindfulness into his approach, and created the Hakomi method. Hakomi Therapists are more mindfulness coaches than therapists.

Hakomi Therapy is a gentle approach that is more a facilitated journey for the client than it is therapy. Rather than giving advice, the therapist guides the client, often through observing his body, to a place of his own release or awareness. A much more organic approach than traditional therapy, a Hakomi therapist will teach the client to be more aware himself, thereby needing therapy less.

Ron Kurtz Hakomi Center
www.ronkurtzhakomi.com
541-482-1714

Hakomi Institute
www.hakomiinstitute.com
888-421-6699

United States Association for Body Psychotherapy
www.usabp.org
202-466-1619

Morita Psychotherapy (mindfulness therapy)
www.todoinstitute.com
802-453-4440

PTSD (Post Traumatic Stress Disorder) Therapy
PTSD and its therapies have become better-known in large part because of our recent wars, starting with the Vietnam War. It was the work of Dr. Peter Levine that brought understanding and effective treatment to PTSD patients. Peter understood it was more physiological than psychological. What he taught me in the early 1980s became a foundation for all my work. You don't need to "understand" the problem, you need to release or complete the stuck trauma. Peter's Somatic Experiencing® is a gentle physical approach to therapy.

Dr. Pat Ogden, an old colleague of mine and former student to Ron Kurtz and Peter Levine, developed Sensorimotor Psychotherapy. Another gentle yet powerful approach to healing the body and mind, Sensorimotor Psychotherapy uses the client's own process and awareness to do the healing.

EMDR (Eye Movement Desensitization and Reprocessing)
Developed to resolve symptoms resulting from disturbing and unresolved life experiences, an EMDR therapist guides the client's eyes as he speaks about the experience. Yes, I know this sounds "woo woo," but it works and it's gentle.

EFT (Emotional Freedom Technique)

EFT is a self-help technique that many therapists and lay people use to release the associated emotion or belief around a word or phrase. EFT involves tapping key acupuncture points while repeating a word that is linked to what you want to shift, as you relax that association.

I was very skeptical at first, but after years of watching the results, I have concluded that these tapping techniques can be very effective. I taught it to my men's group with interesting results. Google "EFT" and you'll find a five-minute how-to video. Free is always good, right?

Somatic Experiencing®
www.somaticexperiencing.com
www.traumahealing.com
303-652-4035

Sensorimotor Psychotherapy Institute (SPI)
www.sensorimotorpsychotherapy.org
800-860-9258

EMDR
EMDR Institute
www.emdr.com
831-761-1040

EFT
EFT Universe
www.eftuniverse.com

Body

Good bodywork can change your life. Beyond the medical model of health, what's the quality of your health? Are you old before your time? Does your body do what you want it to? Are you in pain? How can you be Remarkable if your body is holding you back?

I found that addressing my body issues holistically was both enjoyable and a shortcut to deep change. My first major holistic health and bodywork experience was in 1976. After being convinced by a roommate (a guy who had given up his law practice to train as a Rolfer), I gave Rolfing® (SI) a try. After ten sessions and nine months of integration, I was twenty-five pounds lighter and three-quarters of an inch taller. More than that, I was relaxed for the first time in my life.

I was hooked. I spent the next four years in Boulder, Colorado, learning Rolfing® (SI) and everything else I could learn, including Ron Kurtz's work.

There are so many good forms of bodywork out there, I can't keep track of them any longer. Here are a few of the classics.

Rolfing® (SI)

Rolfing® (SI) was developed by Dr. Ida Rolf in the 1960s as a way to fix structural problems that had been diagnosed "unfixable" by medical doctors. With the counter-culture taking off, Dr. Rolf's work found fertile ground.

Rolfing® (SI) quickly became known for transforming a client's emotional life, too. We store all of our old stress, trauma, and emotions in our body's fascia system (the connective tissue that holds you together). Over time, that tension builds from injury and/or stress, and becomes self-perpetuating. Much of what we think of as unavoidable aging is this cumulative effect of stress. You are your body. If your body is limited, you are limited. Why make it harder on yourself when it can be easy?

When you're tight and stressed, your fascia essentially becomes a suit, covering your body—a suit that is two sizes two small. How well do you move when your clothes are too tight? A tight, misaligned body's quality of functioning decreases, which adds more stress. By releasing that tension, you actually create more room for your skeleton and organs. Remember that lightness you experienced as a kid? You can have that again.

Rolfing® (SI) clients often tell me that after a few sessions, they've gotten more psychological change than from a couple years of psychotherapy. Your mind can't change significantly if your body isn't also changing.

Rolfing® (SI) works best for conditions or goals related to structure, stress, and soft tissue issues. Outside those issues, I recommend other therapies.

When people call me for a recommendation for another Rolfer™, I suggest that they don't see a "gentle Rolfer™," particularly if it's a man. Gentle Rolfing® (SI) is like a light massage and will not work for a man. Good Rolfing® (SI) is like a good stretch—it's uncomfortable at first but it helps you really release.

www.align.org (my site)

Rolf Institute (the certification organization)
www.rolf.org (not all 'Rolfers' are Rolfer—check here to make sure)
800-530-8875

The Feldenkrais Method®

A contemporary of Dr. Rolf, Dr. Moshe Feldenkrais, developed a body therapy that improves your movement through very gentle movements that either you do or someone does to you. The changes might not be as dramatic as Rolfing® (SI), but their scope of practice is wider. They can work with neurological issues that Rolfing® (SI) is generally not effective with. As with Rolfing® (SI), the Feldenkrais Method® work will impact your emotional state.

Feldenkrais Guild
www.feldenkrais.com
800-775-2118

Massage

There are dozens of types of massages. I love massage. You can get some of the results of Rolfing® (SI) over a longer time with a good massage therapist. Don't go for the light, fluffy massage; go for the "therapeutic massage" that really gets in there. It doesn't have to be called "deep tissue" to be good. As with Rolfing® (SI) you should *not* feel beat up afterward! Truthfully, if you are tense it may hurt in the beginning. As you relax, it becomes more pleasurable.

American Massage Therapy Association (AMTA)
www.amtamassage.org
877-905-0577

Acupuncture/Acupressure

After hundreds of years of refinement, and numerous recent scientific studies, you know this works. Using acupuncture and the herbs used in Oriental Medicine, I have seen amazing results with myself and my clients.

Oriental Medicine's scope of practice is the broadest of all these, and its focus is to treat the cause, not just the symptoms. I have seen people cured with Oriental Medicine when their doctors said their conditions were incurable.

With acupressure, rather than using acupuncture needles, practitioners push those same points with their fingers. Like all bodywork, this feels great and can produce sustainable results over time.

National Certification Commission for Acupuncture and Oriental Medicine (NCCAOM®)
www.nccaom.org
904-598-1005

Acupressure has no overseeing organization.

Mind

We limit ourselves with our view that the mind is only the conscious part of us that actively thinks. More than your thoughts, your mind encompasses your beliefs, how you see the world. Also consider what you feed your mind, which includes your own thoughts and what you "consume" mentally (what you read, watch, see, spend time doing, whom you spend time with, etc.)

Coaching

Over the last decade personal coaching has taken off. There are schools that teach it and organizations that "certify" coaches. However, many of the best coaches I know of never took a professional coaching program.

The limitation of some coaching is that it is only that: coaching. Being told what to do and held accountable will produce change. My wish for you is that you are in co-creation with your coach to create what you want. Traditional psychotherapy can spend all the time analyzing the problem. Traditional coaching spends all the time focused on performing.

Pushing through a block will often cause the breakthrough; but other times it can drive the underlying issue deeper. You need a skilled coach who can see this distinction and knows how to work with it so that you not only release that block, but the block stays released.

There are several self-appointed organizations, but no true overseeing organization.

Trainings

Group trainings started in the 1960s with the "encounter groups." They became big business when Werner Erhard created *est* in the 1970s. est got people off their asses. It was a psychological boot camp where the trainers broke participants down, then built them up using their model. Their model of how you should live your life would work better, they claimed, but still it was *their model,* one-size-fits-all. While it has its limitations, I have seen men use the new est, now called Landmark Education Forums, as a catalyst to changing their lives.

Landmark Forum
www.landmarkeducation.com
415-981-8850

Insight Seminars
www.insightseminars.org
800-311-8001

Men's Trainings

The granddaddy of men's training is put on by the ManKind Project (MKP), an international nonprofit that conducts weekend trainings around the world. When I did their New Warrior Training Adventure (NWTA) weekend training in 1995, I was very impressed. There are up to forty participants, with a staff of sixty men, who all pay to be there (except the leader of the weekend). As a nonprofit, no one is making money on this. On the contrary, you have a group of committed men spending a long weekend to make a difference in other men's lives.

Their NWTA is mostly experiential. You don't spend a weekend sitting on your ass. You are having a variety of experiences with men of all ages and backgrounds. Once you complete the training, MKP has a network of men's groups around the world that you can join if you want to. I did the training because I wanted to join one of their groups. These groups can be life changing.

MDI is another nonprofit that has a network of "teams" or groups throughout the United States. It's a smaller organization than MKP, but no less committed. After meeting a few of the leaders of this organization, I can attest to their dedication to helping men. They also sponsor an annual conference that brings together both men and women.

Sterling Institute, a for-profit organization, sponsors weekend trainings for men and women separately. Started in California in 1979, their trainings are conducted on both coasts.

David Deida, author of *The Way of the Superior Man*, conducts workshops for men and women. Deida is provocative. He gets men thinking about who they are in relationship to their purpose, sexuality, and women. He brings spirituality and sexuality to men's work. He irritated me at first, but then I looked beyond his confrontational style of presentation and admitted he was on to something.

Out of the success of our men's groups and from the knowledge I shared in this book, I started Free to Win as a simple, yet powerful way to free men to win as men. The one-day to week-long events we offer utilize small groups of men sitting and participating in activities that liberate them from what has held them back from winning. As this book mentions, the power of a group of men being themselves can't be beat.

I continue to be amazed how a group of strangers in a matter of a few hours can become entirely different men. There's no weird running through the woods naked or psychotherapy techniques used. Its men getting to do what we used to do when we were young: be real. It's remarkable what being real does for a man.

ManKind Project
www.MKP.org
800-870-4611

MDI
www.mdisuccess.com
info@mdisuccess.com

Sterling Institute
www.sterling-institute.com
510- 836-1400

David Deida
www.deida.info
info@deida.info

Free to Win (our company)
www.freetowin.co
info@freetowin.co
206-659-7653

The Vets Journey Home
www.vetsjourneyhome.org
800-236-4692

Men learning to relate to women

If growing or growing up isn't enough motivation to read this book and do the work, maybe women are. Virtually every single man wants to improve his ability to attract the woman he wants. Then, once he "has her," he needs guidance on how to not only keep her, but keep her and himself happy and fulfilled in the relationship.

A new breed of trainings, evolved beyond a "pickup workshop" and focusing on being real, is now popular. The core of these trainings, interestingly, reflects exactly what is taught in this book: that being authentic attracts women with no effort. Rather than learning a set of pickup lines, you learn how to be yourself with women. Simple concept, not always easy to execute; we all have limiting beliefs and behaviors around women.

Men often retreat into their shyness, or expand out into their macho bravado around women. Both are reactions that women don't trust. That's not to say these reactions can't attract a woman; but if you want a real, mature, honest relationship, you need to be real to attract the woman you want in your life.

When men follow the steps outlined in this book, they shift. Their interactions with women shift and their relationship to women also shifts. To shorten and enhance this learning curve, men do these trainings to unlearn unconscious behaviors, and learn how being themselves is a turn-on for a woman.

From watching the videos from the Authentic Men Program (AMP) and having a few men from our groups attend their trainings, I can say that the men and women who put on these trainings are authentic themselves. I have to laugh because it's so obvious that these trainers' biggest passion is not men getting women, it is men getting themselves. They brilliantly use men attracting women as a way to teach men how to be real.

Alison Armstrong started trying to understand men, so that the men she dated would be more to her liking. She realized that the problem wasn't the men, it was her. She needed to grow, she needed to learn to understand men and appreciate them. She built her training business around teaching women how to understand men. She also offers trainings to men about men and women. She is a dynamic and passionate speaker, and I've heard feedback from everyone who has watched her DVDs that it changed their relationships for the better.

Authentic Man Program (AMP)
www.authenticmanprogram.com
415-308-0910

Art of Charm
www.theartofcharm.com
888-413-7177

Alison Armstrong
www.understandmen.com
800-418-9924

Mindfulness Stress Reduction Program

Mindfulness Stress Reduction Program (MSRP) was developed by Dr. Jon Kabat-Zinn in 1979 at the University of Massachusetts Medical School. Being featured in the Bill Moyers' PBS documentary *Healing and the Mind* put it on the map. Today it has grown into an international network of health professionals teaching an eight-week course to kids, prisoners, super-stressed-out Type As, and anyone seeking more clarity.

As I've explained, mindfulness teaches your mind and body to relax, thereby changing your health and life. Anyone can do it—and I mean anyone! When I taught it, there were always men and women who made me wonder if they would stick with it, or get any benefit from the course. In every case they hung in there to receive more than they expected.

Virtually every city has at least one program. Often they are offered at hospitals. Back in the 1990s, when we were the largest provider of Mindfulness courses in Phoenix, Arizona, health insurance paid for the course because of the demonstrable, measurable benefits.

My business partner from my days teaching MSRP is now involved with a proven online mindfulness course taught at emindfulness. Over the years this company mastered teaching mindfulness virtually—it is that simple and easy now.

Center for Mindfulness
www.umassmed.edu/cfm/stress
508-856-2656

emindfulness
www.emindful.com
772-569-4540

Circling

Circling (also known as InterSubjective Meditation) was created by Decker Cunov of the Authentic World as a more active mindfulness practice that you can do with others. It's an experience of connection and understanding of another person's world, celebrating who and where they are in the present moment. You learn how to use curiosity to better understand another person's world and deeply appreciate him or her. This will build your skill of intimacy, which will significantly enhance your relationships. I've seen people learn this and go on to improve their interpersonal and professional relationships.

www.authenticworld.org
888.327.2629

Sexual energy and vitality

Your relationship to sex—including any shame around your sexuality—will have an effect on you. Your vitality is your life force. You can chronologically be an "old man" and be very vital; you can be a young man and chronically fatigued. Your sexual and vital energy affect your creativity, so when you have energy, you want to create and it's easy.

Owning our sexuality is a stretch for most men—too much so for some men, and that's OK. Often working on all the other aspects will profoundly affect your sexuality. Having your body and mind relax will allow you to accept and enjoy your sexuality.

Sexual training organizations usually conduct co-ed trainings. They start at a low level of risk, then progress to higher levels in later trainings. Over the years I have known many men and women who attended these trainings. I can't recall any of them regretting it. Some go to release themselves from shame about their sexuality, others to heal a dysfunction, and some go to improve their relationships or pleasure.

Quodoushka Workshops (the Q) are offered by the Deer Tribe, a group of mixed-blood teachers out of the Native American tradition. They take their task seriously: safety and confidentiality are the cornerstones of their trainings, which are offered around the world. A few years ago, I brought Mukee Okan, one of the Q instructors, to my town for a workshop for our men's group and their partners. She was a hit with both the men and the women. Just speaking about sex was hugely healing.

The Institute for Advanced Study of Human Sexuality is a graduate school approved to train sexologists. There is also the Kinsey Institute at Indiana University, which trains professionals in a more academic manner.

Quodoushka Workshops
www.quodoushka.org

The Institute for Advanced Study of Human Sexuality
www.iashs.edu
415-928-1133

Kinsey Institute at Indiana University
www.kinseyinstitute.org
812-855-7686

Books

The books that started the men's movement:

Iron John: A Book About Men. First published in 1991, author Robert Bly, a poet, wanted to wake men up to what was buried within them. Bly uses Grimm's Fairy Tales and the Wild Man as the metaphor to teach men how to be more than just sensitive or macho. This book started the mythopoetic men's movement.

King, Warrior, Magician, Lover: Rediscovering the Archetypes of the Mature Masculine. Written by Dr. Robert Moore and Douglas Gillette in 1990, this book reads like an academic text. Moore lays out the typology for the four archetypes that is used in much of men's work. They also wrote four books on the structure of male archetypes, based on Jungian psychology, and have CDs available of their work.

Fire in the Belly: On Being a Man. Written by Sam Keen in 1991, this book is an anthem for men to leave the old masculinity behind to find a new relationship with themselves and women.

A Circle of Men: The Original Manual for Men's Support Groups. Written by Bill Kauth, one of the three founders of the ManKind Project, this book lays out the fundamentals of starting a men's group. Kauth's information continues to be relevant today.

Books teaching men to not be women

The Way of the Superior Man, by David Deida, is a quick read on how to leave the macho and sensitive archetypes for what he calls the "third stage man"—a man of purpose. He doesn't focus on giving you many how to's. His intent is to wake you up.

No More Mr. Nice Guy! Psychologist Dr. Robert Glover explains how a nice guy is actually trying to please others while neglecting his own needs. We use this book, as well as Deida's, for new men in our groups to wake up dormant parts of themselves. With so many of us spending more time with women in our youth, we learned to be nice in order to survive. This book can teach you to be nice without giving up yourself.

Christian books

Wild at Heart: Discovering the Secret of a Man's Soul. This Christian version of *Iron John,* written by John Eldredge, challenges Christian men to return to authentic masculinity. Eldredge too is encouraging men to wake up and step out of the cultural fog.

No More Christian Nice Guy: When Being Nice—Instead of Good—Hurts Men, Women, and Children. Paul Coughlin builds on John Eldredge and Robert Glover to give Christian men a how-to manual on being gentle and bold.

Boys to men

Guyland by Dr. Michael Kimmel is a book about young men wanting to hangout as adolescents having fun and not wanting to grow up.

Non-men's books

The Drama of the Gifted Child: The Search for the True Self. Alice Miller explains how as parents we live our incomplete lives through our children, condemning them to the same fate we endured.

The War of Art: Break Through the Blocks and Win Your Inner Creative Battles. Steven Pressfield, author of *The Legend* of *Bagger Vance* and other novels, writes about how to overcome resistance.

Turning Pro: Tap Your Inner Power and Create Your Life's Work. Steven Pressfield's sequel to *The War of Art* is about the inner journey of going from amateur to professional.

The Dip: A Little Book That Teaches You When to Quit (and When to Stick). Seth Godin explains how achievement comes from hanging in through the dip, that tough stretch when there is a lot of work and little reward.

Linchpin: Are You Indispensable? Here Seth Godin tells you how you are indispensable, we need you. Godin gives you a roadmap on how to produce your product or gift so we all can benefit.

The Hero with a Thousand Faces. In this classic, author Joseph Campbell explains through mythology, literature, and history how a person travels through transformation—intended or not.

The Hero's Journey: A Voyage of Self Discovery. Dr. Stephan Gilligan and Robert Dilts use Joseph Campbell's model as the template for deep unconscious change to live a meaningful life.

The Healing Path: A Soul Approach to Illness. Marc Ian Barasch describes his, and others', healing journeys, which parallel the Hero's Journey and Evolutionary Change.

Wherever You Go, There You Are. Dr. Jon Kabat-Zinn lays out what mindfulness is and how to do it in this easy-to-read book.

Focusing. Written by Dr. Eugene Gendlin, the book lays out a simple yet powerful way for you to release emotional and mental restrictions by yourself.

Healing Trauma: A Pioneering Program for Restoring the Wisdom of Your Body. A user-friendly book on trauma from Peter Levine, PhD.

Trauma and the Body: A Sensorimotor Approach to Psychotherapy. The most thorough book on understanding and treating trauma I've read, by Dr. Pat Ogden.

Body-Centered Psychotherapy. Ron Kurtz explains the simple principles of body-centered Hakomi therapy. You will learn how to do this powerful therapy, and you will learn how to better communicate with people.

Rolfing and Physical Reality. Dr. Ida Rolf's book on Rolfing.

Awareness Through Movement: Easy-to-Do Health Exercises to Improve Your Posture, Vision, Imagination, and Personal Awareness. An introduction to the work of Moshe Feldenkrais.

Song of the Deer: The Great Sundance Journey of the Soul. Thunder Strikes, a Native American shaman, wrote this shamanic road map to authenticity.

Movies

Masculine Movies
www.masculinity-movies.com
A blog on movies that inspire men

About Men
www.aboutmenfilm.com
A documentary film about Sandpoint Men's Group

More information

There are a growing number of websites devoted to men. Rather than list them here, go to my blog, www.owenmarcus.com, and look under RESOURCES for more current information, and for websites and blogs on men's issues. If you have a resource you would like to share, please do so at the site. We are in this together.

At my website, I have hundreds of posts concerning men's issues, which, in themselves, could be a valuable resource. I take many of the specific topics of the book and dive deeper into them in these posts, while also giving you resources to explore on your own. You can sign up for the *Toolbox for Change*, a subscription that is more than just a newsletter. You can join the conversation on any post and you can join the community. Use the site—it's free.

Use these resources

If you are stuck in one aspect, give yourself some space to move on, or move around it. If you feel like you can't make any progress in your mind, for example, move your focus to your body, or your spirit.

I offer all this as a guide. Obviously, there is no guarantee that any one suggestion will be the magic bullet. I suggest you explore the ones that appeal to you. Do you feel called to explore your spirituality? Then do it.

If you want to be brave, take on one that is a stretch for you. If the idea of exploring your sexuality terrifies you, you can start there.

In all cases, do your due diligence. Check out the group or person. If you don't have a good feeling, go someplace else. Trust your instincts. The best technique can have mediocre practitioners; conversely, some obscure technique that has a good practitioner who knows what he or she is doing could be exactly what you need. It is very unlikely that any of this could do you any harm, so take a risk. Bottom-line: let your experience be the judge. If you feel safe and it makes some kind of sense, give it three times.

Gratitude

I started my journey thirty-five years ago not out of inspiration, but, as Joseph Campbell describes in his Hero's Journey, out of desperation. My life sucked, and I saw the trajectory I was on was only going to get worse. I stood, lost in my pain, not knowing where to take my first step.

That despair led me to consider options I wouldn't have considered before—before I admitted that I needed to do something different. So when a roommate and recovering attorney sold me on Rolfing® (SI), I had nothing to lose. From that first step I kept stepping forward as others showed up to guide me. In keeping with the Hero's Journey model, new guides continue to show up when I need them.

Some were my challenges, others were my champions. All guided me to the place I am today—for which I am hugely appreciative.

All my clients (both men and women) not only taught me about myself, they taught me what is it is to be human. Their pain, struggle, and triumph showed me what we as humans are capable of achieving. They not only accepted me, they paid me! They allowed me to practice my art on them. It was through working with the men that I learned that men aren't bad or broken; we just never got to learn how to be the man we wanted to be.

Over the years, all the men I have sat with in my men's groups taught me more about what it is to be a man. Their collective wisdom continues to fill the gaps in my maturation. Each week I am amazed at how a man or the group gives a man exactly what he needs. Our group, the Sandpoint Men's Group, continues to deepen and strengthen over the years from each man stepping up. They have my back as I have theirs. The team at Free to Win who is as committed as I am to sharing what we do as I am deserves credit for supporting producing this book and all our work with men.

Much of my work is possible because of the work of other men before me. They taught me and they created an awareness that allows me and other men to move forward. The founders of the men's movement—Robert Bly, Sam Keen, James Hillman, Robert L. Moore, Rich Tosi, and Bill Kauth, along with other men—told both men and women that even though men held power for centuries, we also paid a price.

The well over one hundred men who sat in my groups over the years who were my challengers, supporters and brothers deserve appreciation. Every week I got to experience the power of this new men's work. Every week I saw what men were capable of being. Every week I felt that unique love men give each other when they have a man's back.

Watching the men travel from suffering to succeeding continued to be what keeps me championing our programs and men's groups. Dan Doty a former Sandpoint Men's Group member who returned to New York City to become a successful TV producer is one of a many men who embodies the journey of creation we support. He also is one of my champions who keeps me showing up. So is David Mabelle, another Sandpoint Men's Group alumni.

Asperger's Syndrome, dyslexia, and dyspraxia were my challenging gifts, but I also had amazing parents who never shamed me. They never knew what my struggles were, but they always were at my side. They taught me the value of integrity and compassion through the lives they led.

Through my work with men I learned that few men had the unconditional support I had as a child. Healing my mental disabilities took work. Healing from shame and no support, or even sabotage, can take more.

All my past girlfriends taught me about love, women, and men. It was one, Leslie Villelli, who suggested I write this book. (Many friends over the years have suggested I write a book. This one was the first I wanted to write.)

My editor and friend Theresa Renner took my dyslexic writing and made it into what you read. Her husband, Eldon, is a member of one of my men's groups, so she personally appreciates the work men do in being Remarkable and discovering their unique Masculine Emotional Intelligence. More than anything, her commitment and love made this book a book I'm proud to share with you.

I also want to thank my crowdsourcing proofreaders who graciously volunteered to find the typos, poor grammar and places where something was off: Jake Zmrhal, Daniel Citrome, Scott Edward Anderson, Chris McClellan. I particularly want to thank Charlie Newell an amazing creative man who I met at one of our Two Day Men's Group retreats. Charlie donated an editor to do the finial proof of the book. Drew Dir was that editor who found what others missed to give the manuscript its final polish.

Robert Louis Henry was the man who handled the layout for the manuscript to create an active book, something I don't have the skill or patience to do.

And then there is my friend, Jim Mitchell, who commands attentions much like Samuel L. Jackson, whom I would like to thank. His challenge to men, "Grow the Fuck Up," was the inspiration for my title.

I offer my appreciation to you, the reader, for investing in this book and your own journey of discovery. Please use this book. Use the resources. Go to www.owenmarcus.com to learn more and to communicate with me. Thank you for your trust and time.

Owen Marcus
Sandpoint, ID

Special Bonus for Reading the Book:

Go to www.owenmarcus.com/bookgift to sign up for a free *Toolbox for Men* (more than a newsletter) and receive a special gift for reading the book.

OWEN MARCUS, in healing his Asperger's Syndrome and Dyslexia, learned what it was to be a man. Learning how to be successful as a man, Owen found himself working with other men. His trainings and groups show men how to be free so they may win as men. His blog, www.owenmarcus.com, shares exclusive information on men, women, and relationships. His business, Free to Win—www.freetowin.co, gives men powerful yet fun ways to break out of their boxes to win. He does all this with his neighbors, the moose, and bear in the woods of North Idaho. Owen publishes regular updates of his activities, research, and instigation on Facebook, Google+, and Twitter.

Index

Made in the USA
Middletown, DE
13 June 2020